SMART START

SMART START

The Parents' Complete Guide to Preschool Education

MARIAN EDELMAN BORDEN

Facts On File, Inc.

Smart Start: The Parents' Complete Guide to Preschool Education

Copyright © 1997 by Marian Edelman Borden

Facts On File, Inc.
11 Penn Plaza
New York NY 10001

Library of Congress Cataloging-in-Publication Data

Borden, Marian Edelman.
Smart start : the parents' complete guide to preschool education /
Marian Edelman Borden.
p.   cm.
Includes bibliographical references and index.
ISBN 0-8160-3604-7 (hc). — ISBN 0-8160-3677-2 (pb)
1. Education, Preschool—Parent participation—United States.
2. School choice—United States. 3. Readiness for school—United
States. I. Title.
LB1140.35.P37B67   1997
372.21—dc21   97-11599

Text and cover design by Cathy Rincon

Printed in the United States of America

MP FOF 10 9 8 7 6 5 4 3 2 1

This book is printed on acid-free paper.

For Charles, Sam,

Dan, and Maggie

With all my love

CONTENTS

1 What Kind of Preschool Is Right for Your Child?   1

Montessori, traditional, religious, parent cooperative—what are the philosophical and educational differences among these preschool educational programs? Here is a clear guide that lists the advantages and disadvantages of each program, as well as guidelines for choosing the location, schedule, and frequency of classes. There is a full discussion of whether a mainstream school is the best choice for your physically or emotionally handicapped child; whether twins should attend the same school and class; and how to make an educational choice for a chronically ill child. Worried about how you can afford preschool tuition bills? Here are the answers you need to have *before* you look at preschools.

2 The ABC's of Choosing a Preschool   27

Here is a step-by-step guide for observing and selecting the right preschool for your child. It includes a detailed checklist for judging programs, facilities, and teaching staff. Learn the nonquantifiable qualities that you should include in your evaluation (is the classroom gender neutral?) and the not-so-secret quality that every good preschool teacher must have (*hint: do you know any knock-knock jokes?*).

3 The Day-Care Dilemma   60

Many parents need full-time day care, but also want a developmentally appropriate preschool program. Here's how to make sure that your child has both. This chapter tells you what your child will learn in day care and how it supplements her preschool education. There are tips for finding the right kind of child care for your family and effective ways to ease communication between school, day care, caregiver, and parents. This chapter will suggest ways to make it all work.

4 Ready, Set, Go: The Opening Days of School   84

School opens and is your child ready? Yes. Check out the parent-tested suggestions for dealing with all the issues that surround the opening days of school. You will find answers to these questions: Who should take the child to school? How can you smooth the transition from home to class? Should parents stay in the classroom for the first few days? How can you reduce separation anxiety (for parents and child!)?

5 What's Happening at School?   111

Some children are full of information; others can't—or won't—share what happens at school. This chapter will provide a glimpse into the average day in a nursery school. It will also give parents an insight into why their child is so tired, cranky, or wired up after a great day at school. Learn why playing with blocks may help your child pass an advanced physics class in high school. Here are some conversational gambits that will encourage parent-child discussion.

Meeting your child's teacher for a conference can be a daunting experience, even though you are discussing your favorite topic—your child. Learn what to expect from the teacher and what both of you should bring to the conference table to get the most from a preschool conference. Sometimes even the best planning doesn't work out. When your child is very unhappy in school, you'll want to figure out what's causing the problem. Here are techniques for discovering whether it is bad chemistry with the teacher, the class, or the program. Is it a problem outside of school (even if he is expressing it as "hating school")? Is it something new or a long-term problem. Here are the symptoms of child abuse and what you must do to help your youngster.

Your child will change dramatically, physically, emotionally, and intellectually, during his preschool years—and his school's curriculum should meet those different needs. Learn what you can expect from a preschooler at each age—and what you can do at home to supplement your child's education. On the health front there is a guide to preschool health problems. Preschool is a breeding ground for viruses—here's why, as well as some tips to prevent your child from getting sick.

Learn what teachers mean when they talk about "kindergarten readiness." It's more than whether your child knows his letters and numbers: here is a checklist of the intellectual, physical, and emotional signs that your child is ready for elementary school. If your child has a birthday close to the cutoff date for kindergarten entry, you'll want to know your options. There is a full discussion of alternatives such as transition classes, repeating the four-year-old class, or just taking a chance.

Explore the best ways to encourage a lifelong love of learning.

Appendix 1
Preschool Evaluation Sheet   200

Appendix 2
Recommended Childhood Immunization Schedule   204

Appendix 3
Resources (including Internet web sites for preschool parents)   207

FOREWORD

The preschool years are magic. I say that with fading recollections of potty-training struggles, temper tantrums, and wearying fatigue. But the sweet memories of my children discovering the world anew linger in my mind. Children between the ages of two and five approach the world with a sense of wonder they rarely experience again.

As parents of a preschooler, you are witness to changes that occur at an almost dizzying pace. In three short years, your child will develop from a barely verbal, toddling infant to a walking, talking "real" person. Of course you want to maximize your youngster's opportunities for development, but most of all, you want to enjoy this very special time. *Smart Start* will help you understand what is happening during these exciting years. It will help you build an effective partnership between preschool and home, one that enriches your child's life.

Ask me some of the childhood highlights of my five children and I can recall their athletic achievements, scholastic accomplishments, endless extracurricular activities. But those obvious milestones were built on the self-esteem that was being nurtured in the early years. I remember with striking clarity—and a smile—that look of triumph on my two-year-old firstborn's face as he emerged from his room to inform me that he had dressed himself. No doubt the fashion police might have questioned his choices, but in that small act of independence was built the foundation of his later achievements. It was a quiet victory, but an important one. When I didn't change a single item of his mismatched clothes, Peter learned that his mother believed in his ability to make choices, to try and succeed.

The ultimate measure of successful parenting is whether you raise a child with a positive self-concept—that is, a youngster who likes himself, who feels good about the unique individual that he is, who has an honest assessment of his strengths and abilities, and who accepts himself and others. We nurture that self-esteem from the day the baby is born. Just like a house is only as strong as its foundation, the messages we give to our children in the early years are even more important than the ones they will hear from us during adolescence.

To reinforce a child's self-esteem, as parents, we must give him opportunities to explore the world around him; we must encourage him to try new things, to take risks. We must applaud his successes and reassure him that failure is okay too. No one ever fails without learning something valuable. Our role as parents is to model for our children what it's like to feel the fear and then "go for it" anyway. That's what parents must instill in their children during the early years.

And a good preschool program reinforces what you are doing at home. That word of encouragement from the teacher about a job well done when Jamie distributes the snacks or an "I'm proud of you for caring" to Philip when he attempts to help a classmate in distress teaches your child that he is valued, that he is important, that he is capable, and that he can trust the world around him.

Several years ago, when we were taking our third child off to college—our first to go out of state—my husband said he had but three words of advice for her. My immediate thought was that he meant *call me anytime*, but instead he advised *figure it out*. And that's what all those years of parenting had been about. We want, at home and in the schools they attend, to imbue our youngsters with the appropriate personal tools and skills to enable them to solve life's problems in our absence some day. No parent can ever hope to leave a child at college having specifically prepared her for every eventuality she may face. Nevertheless, we can realistically impart to our youngsters during their childhood some fundamental keys to personal success. What must we do at home and look to a preschool to do?

✎ If we, the adults in our children's lives, give them a positive self-image, confidence that they can indeed "figure it out," then they will be better prepared to do just that.

✎ If we model self-discipline and place limits on behavior during the preschool years and childhood, then we can hope that our youngsters will internalize those traits into self-control and self-discipline.

✎ If we model respect for others, insist on respect for siblings, parents, family members, and if our teachers insist on respect for classmates and the school community, then we teach our children not only to respect all people but to expect—and demand—that respect for themselves.

✎ If we allow our children to experience the natural consequences of their actions, even if it is at times painful or messy, then we give them the skills to think through problems and weigh potential outcomes.

✎ If parents and preschool identify and model important personal and ethical values, then our children incorporate these values into their daily lives.

✎ If we promote a positive attitude in life, then we teach our children the importance of hope and hard work.

The commitment of parents and teachers to building this solid foundation in early childhood results in young adults able to cope with any situation they might encounter.

What can you expect a good preschool program to provide your child? The variety of activities available, the nurturing your child receives from other adults, the interaction with other children all help your youngster to develop physically, emotionally, and intellectually. Such opportunities will help build the skills she will need to cope with life.

And it's not an insignificant contribution that the time a child spends in a nursery school program gives parents an opportunity to recharge. Preschool is also an opportunity for parents to meet other families with youngsters the same age. Parents quickly discover that sharing child-rearing experiences and concerns with other adults is one of the surest ways to save parental sanity.

But most of all, a good preschool program doesn't measure its success by how many of its participants eventually enter Harvard or, even, enter kindergarten with the ability to read. Rather, a strong preschool curriculum reflects a commitment to the young child and the conviction that childhood is a precious time that should not be hurried. As you read *Smart Start* you'll find the tools you will need to "figure it out" and to choose the right program for your child.

I believe that parents can—and should—enjoy every age of their child. There are magical moments throughout what is an all-too-brief time when our youngsters are living at home with us. But the preschool years of my five children will always hold a special place in my heart. As I remember looking at the world through the open, trusting, inquisitive eyes of young children, as I recall their rose-colored glasses, their unquenchable optimism, their excitement about even the most mundane chores in life, my faith in the future is ever renewed.

—Marianne Egeland Neifert, M.D., "Dr. Mom"
  Author of *Dr. Mom's Parenting Guide* and *Dr. Mom: A Guide to Baby and Child Care*

PREFACE

This year, more than 2.5 million children will be enrolled in nursery schools, more than half in privately funded programs. Preschools were once an option, even a luxury, for families. Just 25 years ago many children stayed at home until they entered kindergarten—or even first grade, socializing with their siblings, the neighborhood kids, or just Mom. But today, most youngsters attend some kind of preschool program. Teachers expect the child to enter kindergarten having experienced the socializing and educational experience of nursery school. For you the question then becomes: How can I make sure that my child's first school experience is the very best it can be?

The answer is important because the one, two, or three years your child spends in preschool will be his first introduction to formal education. A good preschool program teaches children that learning is fun; that school is a warm, welcoming, nonjudgmental place; that teachers are there to help, never hurt, you.

This parent-to-parent guidebook will lead you step by step through the preschool experience of your child. It is practical and detailed, ranging from the philosophical to the pragmatic.

My credentials to write this book are fourfold, and their names are Charles, Sam, Dan, and Maggie—my kids. They're what motivated me to start researching the topic. In the 10 years I have been involved with preschool, I've seen teachers who made a real difference in my child's life. I have also endured some who were benign. I've seen programs that were exciting and the "learning from doing" was amazing; I've also seen programs that were boring and the kids were just marking time.

So I began talking to other parents, teachers, and early childhood specialists about how to maximize the preschool experience for young children and their parents. This book is the result. It will give you the basic educational theory you need to know in order to make an informed choice, as well as provide you with the practical advice of other parents about how to help your child through these formative years. And because school isn't exclusively about education, there are chapters on what's happening physically, emotionally, and intellectually to your preschooler.

Besides the strong educational and emotional rationale for this book, there is also a very practical reason. Preschool is the first educational investment parents will make. In some urban areas, preschool tuition can be as high as $10,000 per year—for a half-day program! Today when the emphasis is on value received for the dollar, *Smart Start* is designed to make sure that parents are spending their money wisely.

Now for some notes and thanks.

As the mother of three sons and one daughter, I am firmly committed to gender equality. The issue of which pronoun to use when writing is always troubling, so I alternated throughout the text when referring to young children. Reality about child-care workers, however, compelled me to use the feminine pronoun as more than 98 percent of all childcare workers are women. I have many people to thank: first, and always, my husband, John, my life partner, who supported this project, offered advice, perspective, editorial suggestions, and most importantly, has always shared parenting responsibilities. To Charles, Sam, Dan, and Maggie, I am indebted. You are my inspiration.

Special thanks to the many parents from around the country who contributed to this book. Your honesty and perspective will help make the preschool experience much easier for other families.

I am very grateful to Mary Goldman, Sara Arnon, Hannah Holsten, Wendy Brooks, the staff of the Montessori Teacher Training Center, Elizabeth Silverstone, Joan MacFarlane, Amy Keltz, and Kate Kelly Schweitzer for their invaluable advice. Many thanks to the always helpful staff at the Larchmont Public Library, especially Jacqui Anderson, Nancy Manion, Bernadette McGuire, Ray Messing, and Cindy Rocchio.

To those parents about to begin the search for a preschool, good luck. It's a new and exciting period for your child and you. Enjoy this time—it passes all too quickly.

WHAT KIND OF PRESCHOOL IS RIGHT FOR YOUR CHILD?

The process of choosing the right preschool for your child begins months, perhaps even years, before the first day of class. In fact, some of the decisions you will make have less to do with any one specific school and more about the needs of, and the kind of education you want for, your child.

✎ Montessori or Piaget curriculum?
✎ Public or private program?
✎ Affiliated with a church/synagogue or secular?
✎ Full- or half-day program? extended day-care hours?
✎ Partial- or full-week program?
✎ Single or multiage grouping?

There are, of course, certain standards, like those that have to do with safety or teacher/child ratio, on which you should not compromise. But there are many other issues, which are a matter of personal choice, for which you, the parent, will have to decide what is best for your child, what you feel is essential, what can be compromised. During the process of reading about early childhood education and visiting specific programs, you should develop a checklist of those

> **TIP:** Choosing a preschool is a personal decision —one that has to be a good match for your child, and for you. You should make your decision after thinking about your own educational philosophy, considering your family's lifestyle, and trying to match your child's personality and needs to the programs that you have seen.

qualities that you want in a school. You should prioritize them so that the program you select for your child will meet at least the most important of the standards on your list.

It's possible that, after much thought and several visits, you decide that the quality of a specific program is so outstanding that you are willing to put aside certain criteria. For example, while you might prefer to send your child to a religiously affiliated program, you discover a local secular school is a better match. Or you might find that although you and a friend with a child of the same age are trying to choose a school for both children, a certain program will be perfect for one child, and not as good a fit for another.

The Educational Theories of Preschools

Even before you check out the hours, the cost, and the playground, you will need to make a basic decision about the *educational philosophy* you want in the preschool you choose for your child. Any high quality program is committed to the physical, intellectual, social, and emotional growth of young children—*how* to achieve those goals will vary. A school develops its curriculum based on different educational theories about how young children learn. You want to select a program that is compatible with your own child-rearing philosophy *and* your child's needs. This is important because a basic compatibility between school and home will avoid confusing your child, reduce unreasonable parental expectations, and facilitate parent-teacher communication. You want your child to hear the same messages at home and at school.

You will find that most preschools base their curriculum on one of two main educational models: Piaget or Montessori. You will see differences between the Piaget and Montessori philosophies in the role of the teacher in the classroom, the theory of how young children learn and how to stimulate their intellectual and physical growth, the importance of free play, the value of dramatic play, the merit of group activities, the benefits of art projects, and the toys and materials available in the classroom.

There are other educational models including the Waldorf, or Rudolf Steiner Schools, and Progressive Schools (see Glossary). While these schools each have their own curriculum, they share with both Piaget and Montessori a developmental approach to learning. Understanding the basic educational models will give you a framework for approaching preschool education.

The school director should be able to articulate the underlying educational philosophy of her program. There are clear differences between traditional Piaget-based programs and the Montessori approach. But actions speak louder than words. You will want to see, during your school visit, how the theory is translated into the types of activities planned for the children and the toys and

SUPPOSE I DON'T HAVE A CHOICE

Perhaps you live in a community where there are limited choices for preschools, where, for example, the only nearby program is based on the Montessori model. Is it still important to understand the other approaches to preschool education? Yes! Understanding the theoretical and philosophical underpinnings of these models will help you focus on what educational ideas and activities you feel are essential for your child's development. You may then choose to encourage your own school to include them or to find ways yourself to supplement your child's experience.

In the next few pages, we'll review the educational differences in approach between Piaget-based preschools and Montessori early childhood programs. But no matter what a school calls itself, or what is written in the glossiest brochure, your personal observation of the programs is critical.

materials available. Even within the same philosophical approach, in different schools you will find different emphases, stricter or more flexible interpretations of the model.

Piaget Curriculum

Traditional nursery schools, as distinct from Montessori schools, base much of their educational philosophy on the theories of Jean Piaget, a Swiss psychologist (1896–1980), although the work of other educational leaders such as John Dewey and Arnold Gesell greatly influence modern preschool curriculum.

You may also hear terms such as "open classroom," and "whole child approach" to describe traditional nursery school programs. Within this category you may find: half-day programs (some with extended hours); full-day schedules; church/synagogue-affiliated programs; independent schools (also called private schools); lab schools (affiliated with and staffed by professors and students of the education department of a university); and some public prekindergarten (pre-K) schools including Head Start. Generally, the Piaget school is organized by age, with separate classes for twos, threes, and fours.

Piaget theorized that children, from birth through age 12, pass through four progressive cognitive stages of mental development. These stages are at least partially independent of a child's chronological age, and children progress through them at different rates. *It is this emphasis on "developmentally appropriate" activities, rather than focusing on chronological age, that is key to this educational philosophy.* Underlying this approach is understanding how young children learn—and then developing an appropriate curriculum.

Piaget studied the intellectual development of young children and concluded that preschoolers learn about their world through their senses. They explore and understand what they can see, hear, touch, taste, and smell. They learn through doing.

For example, how will a young child learn about shapes: round, square, triangle? In a Piaget-based preschool, a young child

4

learns about shapes through a variety of experiences and with a multitude of materials. Besides any books that the teacher might read to the class about shapes, any songs the group might sing ("The wheels on the bus go round and round"), during free-play time, the preschooler might build with round, square, and triangular blocks. After building with them, she learns during cleanup time how to organize the blocks by shape, putting the round ones on one shelf, the square blocks on another. During cooking, she might bake round cookies. During art, the preschooler might paste down circles to form a snowman, adding a rectangular shape for the hat and a triangle for a nose. During playground time, she might kick a ball, swing on a hanging tire, go down a slide—each of these activities involves shapes.

The opportunities for learning are endless and never involve a teacher in the front of the class with the students seated at desks. According to Piaget, that is not how preschoolers learn, and a high quality preschool develops a curriculum that offers a richness of materials and experiences for the young child.

The Importance of Play

Piaget believed that children learn through play. The various centers in the classroom, a book corner, housekeeping/dress-up area, blocks, art, games, all have developmentally appropriate materials, which encourage the youngsters to experiment and grow through their play. There is no "right" way to use materials, and children are encouraged to experiment and invent new ways to use them.

In a traditional preschool class, the teacher will serve as the catalyst to spark the children's interest and participation in developmentally appropriate activities. The curriculum is planned to permit the young child to discover knowledge. This is sometimes described as "discovery learning," as opposed to instruction. Piaget advocates believe that the young child will grow physically, intellectually, socially, and emotionally, as he tries new things within a play context. The emphasis is on learning to function independently, developing social skills, and building self-esteem.

Academics, in the traditional sense, are a by-product of the development of these other areas.

Walk into the traditional nursery school class and you will probably find a noisy bustle of activity with some children playing in groups, while others are working individually. As you look around the room you'll discover some children will be in the block corner constructing a city; others will be in the housekeeping area having a tea party; another group may be working on the art project of the day; while individual youngsters may be looking at books, feeding the class guinea pig, or painting at an easel. There may be group projects (such as painting a mural or a class trip); there may be group times (such as circle time first thing in the morning or story time); but a significant part of the day in a Piaget curriculum is for *free play*, where the child chooses which activity or area she wants. Some schools may make even group time optional, with a child having free choice (within safety limits) during the entire class.

Montessori Curriculum

Maria Montessori (1870–1952), an Italian physician-educator, also believed in a developmental approach to learning, but within a specially prepared environment and with teachers who have been trained in the Montessori method. Reading, writing, and counting are incorporated in the Montessori curriculum, but specially designed Montessori materials and learning sequences are used to teach these more academic subjects.

Why Multiage?

Unlike a traditional nursery school, the concept of mixed ages is key to the Montessori method. A class may have threes, fours, fives, even sixes, with the older children serving as teachers/mentors to the younger ones. The multiage grouping is based on the concept of creating a family-like atmosphere where learning occurs naturally, with the more experienced child teaching the less experienced one. Serving as mentor/teacher also reinforces the older child's own knowledge. Multiage groups also work, Montessori believed, because children of the same age may be at different developmental levels. A perfectly bright four-year-old may have the small-motor skills of a three-year-old, while a two-year-old may be ready for some three-, even four-year-old activities. The multiage classroom permits each child to progress at his own pace. Many Montessori teachers believe that young children first entering the program have an easier adjustment because they have the older students to help them. There is never an entire class of new students.

Like the Piaget model, the Montessori schools may be organized into half-day programs (some with extended hours); full-day schedules; church/synagogue-affiliation; independent schools (also called private schools); and some public pre-K schools including Head Start.

"Freedom Within Limits"

In a Montessori program, the activities are child directed, rather than teacher driven. According to Montessori precepts, the child will initiate those activities and use those materials that interest her, for as long as she wishes. The classroom operates on the principle of "freedom within limits."

Children may work on their own, or with other children, at their own pace. The primary interaction is *not* between the teacher and child, but rather between the child and self-correcting materials. The teacher serves as a resource to provide the materials that are appropriate for the child's level, and to demonstrate the correct use.

The Montessori classroom may be quieter than one found in a traditional nursery program. The children are focused on their own chosen activity for longer periods of concentration.

Montessori Sensory Materials

The Montessori materials are an essential part of the program. They are to be used in special ways and in specific sequences, and are designed to teach numbers, letters, and abstract ideas. While the underlying premise is similar to Piaget's concept of *sensory education*, the Montessori method believes that a structured context is essential for the young child's development. The materials were conceived to stimulate the child's senses and permit her to act as her own "teacher."

Stimulating the visual sense, there are instructional materials such as wooden blocks graduated in size with which a child can build a tower, learning through trial and error to put the largest on the bottom and successively smaller sizes on the top. There are round cylinders and wooden prisms that similarly teach the concepts of ordered classification from small to large; extreme and small differences; fine gradations.

To appeal to a young child's sense of touch, Montessori developed a variety of interesting instructional materials. For example, there is a collection of fabric, two pieces each of velvet, satin, silk, wool, cotton, and coarse and fine linen. Using a blindfold, a child must find the matching pieces of fabric, learning in the process the concept of same and different. Or having observed that young children often recognize an object from feeling it, again blindfolded, a student must, based on touching the object, recognize and call out the name of various shapes such as sphere, prism, pyramid, cone, and cylinder. Having learned about shapes, the child can then transfer that knowledge to shapes of larger objects—for example, recognizing that a school bus is a cylinder with four spheres.

To stimulate the child's sense of hearing, there is a Montessori-designed series of closed cylinders that contain varying materials. The child must then match the *sounds* that are produced when each cylinder is shaken. There are smelling vials to stimulate the olfactory sense and tasting exercises to foster the gustatory sense.

Montessori Academic Materials

Once the child has mastered the simpler instructional materials, he can move on to the ones that might be described as more "academic." There are Montessori materials to encourage reading, writing, and counting. For example, there is a sequence of learning materials that helps the young child write. There are tracing insets of different shapes, which the young child can use to help develop the small-motor control necessary for writing. The teacher and child will use a series of boxes that contain the letters of the alphabet, usually covered in sandpaper, to practice the sounds of the letters. He will then trace with his finger the sandpaper letters (note: the different textures are part of the sensory experience). When he has mastered the sounds of the letters, and finger tracing while identifying the letter, he will move on to printing the letters with a pencil. Eventually, the child can combine the letters to make words and learn to read the words he has written. The Montessori approach allows the child to move, at his own rate, from the strictly sensory through the abstract concepts, with support from the materials, teacher, and his own peers. Montessori also has materials and sequences for teaching number concepts.

Daily Chores as Part of Program

Montessori believed that fostering a child's self competence in daily tasks encourages his sense of independence and she designed materials to help. For example, there is a group of Montessori-designed wooden frames to which pieces of fabric or leather are attached and can be buttoned, zipped, hooked, etc. With practice, the child learns how to dress and undress himself. This personal competence carries over to the classroom. Students wash the tables, sweep the floor, pick up the materials, and return them to their designated areas.

Order is very important in the classroom as Maria Montessori believed that just as children organize and classify their experiences, the classroom should have a clear and orderly design. This need for order is also part of the underlying premise of the Montessori approach: respect between teacher and child; among peers; for the classroom environment. Children are expected to care for the classroom, return materials to the proper place, and in the process develop a sense that they are contributing to the creative, inviting atmosphere of learning.

While a Montessori classroom may look similar to many other preschool classrooms, there are important differences. The Montessori materials will each be stored in its own specific place, visible and within easy reach of children. Depending on how strictly the school follows the Montessori philosophy, except for easel painting, there may be no special art activities. While music, storytelling, and movement are part of the Montessori curriculum, fantasy play, in a strict Montessori classroom, is not encouraged, and there will probably not be a dress-up corner.

Although Piaget-based preschools may have strong parent participation, Montessori preschools have an organized program for parents to understand and participate in the learning process.

A WORD OF CAUTION

Montessori is a word in the public domain. Any school may call itself Montessori regardless of its curriculum. Further, some Montessori preschools follow a stricter interpretation of the curriculum than others. The school visit becomes even more critical as you decide if the Montessori method, as interpreted by your local school, is appropriate for your child. According to the American Montessori Society (AMS), to be an authentic Montessori classroom, the school should have:

✏ Teachers educated in the Montessori philosophy and methodology for the age level they are teaching. For a full AMS credential, Montessori teachers must have a minimum of a full year of Montessori training following the baccalaureate degree (BA) including a year's student teaching under supervision.

✏ A partnership established with each child's family. The tri-part relationship—school-parents-child—is considered an integral part of the individual child's total development.

✏ A multiaged, multigraded, heterogeneous grouping of students.

✏ A diverse set of Montessori materials, activities, and experiences that are designed to foster physical, intellectual, creative, and social independence.

✏ A schedule that allows large blocks of time to problem-solve, to see connections in knowledge, and to create new ideas.

✏ A classroom atmosphere that encourages social interaction for cooperative learning, peer teaching, and emotional development.

COMPARING PIAGET AND MONTESSORI

Piaget

Teacher	No national requirements for certification, but prefer teachers with undergraduate/graduate degrees in early childhood education
Age Grouping	Separate classrooms for twos, threes, and fours
Materials	Chosen by each preschool, generally organized into activity corners including housekeeping, art, music, science, blocks, reading
Curriculum	Varies but generally is teacher directed; teacher serves as catalyst for classroom activities

Montessori

Teacher	For certification, must have undergraduate or graduate degree in early childhood education plus certification from Montessori teacher-training program
Age Grouping	Multiage grouping is essential part of program, may group twos, threes, fours, and even fives together
Materials	Specific Montessori-developed materials are integral part of curriculum
Curriculum	"Child directed" with emphasis on "freedom within limits"

Types of Preschool

Full Day or Half Day?

You will want to consider the age and energy level of your child when choosing between a half-day or full-day program, and whether you want or need extended hours after the regular school day ends. A full-day program generally conforms to regular school hours (usually 9 A.M. to 3 P.M.), but some schools arrange additional hours before or after school to meet the demands of working parents.

> **TIP:** If you decide a full-day program better meets your child's and your own needs, ask how the school handles rest time. Many build in a quiet time after lunch when the children may rest on mats (many actually fall asleep) or at least play or look at books quietly.

You may want to increase the length of the program as your child gets older, perhaps starting off with a half-day schedule for young preschoolers, twos and threes, and switching to a full day or at least an extended day program for fours and fives. If you live in an isolated area or where arranging activities or play dates during nonschool hours would be difficult, you may decide that your child would benefit from a longer program. In this case, you need to balance the advantages and disadvantages of long hours and your own particular family situation. If it is clear that your child would do better with shorter school hours, but you need additional coverage, you may decide to combine a half-day program with some kind of at-home baby-sitting or day-care arrangement.

Even if you have a high-energy level child, one who seems to be on the run almost constantly or who is looking for another play date before the first one has left, don't underestimate how demanding a preschool program can be. Besides the physical requirements of an exciting, high-quality program that has a strong outdoor playground component, there is also the psychological stress. Consider that a preschool day requires a young child to separate from her parents/caregiver, maintain her composure, learn to share adult attention and materials, focus on new tasks and activities, interact with peers, and cope with self-competency issues like dressing and toileting. This is a lot for a young child to sustain over a long period of time. It's the reason why many preschoolers, those who have long ago given up their daily naps, may come home from preschool and either sleep or need a quiet rest period in the afternoon. Preschoolers need the "down" time.

Morning or Afternoon Program?

Choosing between a morning or afternoon program may be easy if your community offers only one or the other. But many popular schools offer families a choice, both as a way to meet a demand for space, as well as to fit individual family schedules. Sometimes, schools offer a combination program, for example, the child attends school one morning and two afternoons. And some schools offer, for an additional fee, the option of extended hours. For example, the regular school day is from 9 A.M. to 12 noon, but you can enroll your child for a lunch program that lasts until 2 P.M., one or more days during the week. You will probably find that some children in the class will end the day at noon, while others may elect to stay for the lunch program only once a week, while still others will stay for lunch every day.

To make a decision, consider your own family's habits and needs. For some families, half the day is already gone by nine in the morning. If your child is an early riser, then you may prefer a morning program. Especially for younger preschoolers who are still napping in the afternoon, a morning activity, followed by an afternoon rest makes sense.

On the other hand, if your child often doesn't rouse until nine, then you may prefer to take it easy in the morning and elect an afternoon program. One family, where both parents worked late, deliberately chose an afternoon program because they wanted their child to stay up with them in the evenings. The child's daily schedule then became a late start in the mornings (a baby-sitter came into the home while the parents worked), followed by school in the afternoon, and then a short nap late in the day. Although initially concerned about the transition to a morning program for kindergarten, the parents were delighted when the change was surprisingly easy. Although bedtime was moved to an earlier time, as the youngster grew older he also needed less sleep and was easily able to get up in the morning.

Another family felt that it was always easy to pass the morning hours. By the time morning chores around the house were finished, perhaps a quick trip to the supermarket, library, etc., it was time for lunch and then afternoon was school. This family found that a morning program meant a long afternoon and a full schedule of either planned activities or play dates.

There are other practical considerations to weigh in scheduling your child's program.

✎ **Car pools** If arranging car-pool transportation is important, check with your neighbors before signing up. Similarly, some programs offer bus transportation for a fee, but it may only be available for either the morning or afternoon session.

✎ **Friends** Although your child will certainly make new friends in class, it may ease the transition to walk into the classroom and connect immediately with some familiar faces. You may want to coordinate his schedule with his friends.

✎ **Adult friends** You may choose to enroll your child in a certain session because your friends have chosen that time slot. This can be helpful if you need backup coverage in case of emergencies.

✎ **Climate** On a very practical level, if you live in an area where outdoor play is difficult by midafternoon, you may prefer to schedule a morning program to be sure that your youngster can enjoy playground time and still be inside during the heat of the day.

✎ **Family/work schedule** If your own schedule demands the family is up and out, to make trains, go to work, take older children to school, appointments, shopping, etc., then a morning program may be preferable.

✎ **Child care** Your child-care provider may have a preference. If she is responsible for other school-age children, she may prefer that everyone be on the same schedule.

How Many Days a Week?

In the 1960s and 1970s, when most preschool programs began at age three, the younger children went to school two, perhaps three mornings per week, and then graduated to a five-day program for the four-year-old class. But today, as we have moved back the age when many preschool programs begin, it is the two-year-old class that meets just a couple of times a week, and by age three, many young children are ready for a five-day program.

Again, you need to assess your own family's needs and your child's energy levels. Given a quality preschool program, most young children can adapt well to whichever schedule you choose.

JUST PUTTERING AROUND

Don't underestimate the value of "puttering time." You don't need to feel that you have to fill every moment of your child's day with scheduled activities such as gym, swim, dance, or art classes. If you choose to send your child to a less than full-time schedule, and elect to have her spend some mornings or afternoons with you or your caregiver, don't worry that you will adversely affect your child's social or cognitive development.

Church/Synagogue-Affiliated Schools

You may choose to send your child to a preschool program that incorporates religious instruction into the curriculum. Be sure to ask, and preferably observe, how the school includes the religious components into their daily or weekly program. Remember that some schools are merely housed in church/synagogue buildings, but have no connection to the religious movement. Others limit the religious component to holidays, while still others include daily prayers as part of the preschool day, and may celebrate only holidays particular to that religion. For example, you may want to ask a school affiliated with a synagogue if they celebrate Halloween or Valentine's Day. Although many would consider these secular holidays, more observant Jewish preschools may not permit their observance because their origins are found in non-Jewish religions.

You will want to check the qualifications of the teaching staff. Some schools may consider religious observance more important than educational training or experience. While you may prefer that the preschool teacher be of the same religion as the affiliated church/synagogue, many good programs hire qualified teachers who then learn the religious components of the school's curriculum.

Advantages

What are the advantages of sending your child to a preschool affiliated with your religion?

✎ Children become more familiar and comfortable with the traditions and customs of their heritage.

✎ If your family is observant, having your child in an affiliated preschool reinforces what is being taught at home and facilitates observance of holidays and customs.

✎ If your family is not observant, having your child in this type of preschool often helps to build a place for religion in the family structure. Many parents believe that having a child in a church/synagogue preschool forced them to focus on religious issues they had ignored and gave them a welcoming community in which to sort out these issues.

Disadvantages

The main disadvantages of a church/synagogue preschool are:

✎ Lack of diversity. Most, if not all classmates, will share the same religious background, which means that your child may not be exposed to a variety of customs, traditions, language, or experiences.

✎ Conflicting value systems. If your family is either less or more religiously observant than the school, your child may find the contrast between home and school difficult to understand. Much depends on both your own and the school's attitude and how each of you deal with the differences. Some programs are comfortable and used to dealing with the issue, others may be more judgmental or even evangelical.

Parent Cooperatives

In these types of nursery schools, much of the support structure of the program depends on parent volunteers. In some schools parents must volunteer in the classroom, serving as teaching assistants on a regular basis. In other schools, parents do not normally work in the classroom, but fill all other roles such as administrative tasks, lunchroom volunteers, fund-raising, bookkeeping, or maintenance.

Advantages

There are three main advantages of this type of preschool:

1. Cooperative preschools are generally less expensive than other comparable programs.
2. Preschool volunteers often discover a strong sense of community and friendship.
3. Your child learns very early an important lesson: education is a family issue. Your child will clearly see the family-school partnership.

Disadvantages

The main disadvantages of cooperative preschool programs are:

1. Time—or lack of it. Because of work, family, financial, and/or personal pressures, it is often difficult to find volunteers who will be available on a regular basis. Even with the best of intentions, many parents simply have no idea of the time commitment they are making when they elect to use a cooperative preschool and may be unable to fulfill their time pledges. If you are conscientious about your volunteer commit-

IF IT IS NOT YOUR RELIGION

Sometimes you may decide that the best school for your child is affiliated with a house of worship that is not of your religion. You may think the program is significantly better; the location is more convenient; carpooling is possible. Whatever the reason, you have to be prepared for dealing with the obvious conflict between home and school. It's unreasonable for you to expect the school to change their program because of your choice, but you should certainly discuss the issue with the director and teachers. You should expect tolerance and acceptance of differences within the classroom. Your child will have questions, and you must be prepared to discuss why your family does not observe the holidays celebrated in school or participate in the religious events of the institution. It may be difficult for your child to reconcile the differences, but with understanding and support, it can be and has been done.

ments, you may find yourself picking up the slack for those who are not. Before joining a program, get a realistic idea of how effectively the voluntary schedule works.

2. Who serves? You will want to know if a parent must fulfill the obligation or whether substitutes such as nannies, grandparents, aunts, uncles, etc., can complete the family's duties. Will it bother you if you are the only parent working? Were you looking for a way to belong to a community? If the jobs are being completed by au pairs, will you feel cheated from the opportunity to make new adult friends and meet other preschool parents? If you have an au pair or nanny, will she feel comfortable working with other parents?

3. If the school uses parents to staff or assist in the classroom, the teacher's aides may not necessarily be qualified—or even very interested. Ask the director how the classroom help is chosen—and what, if any, is the effect on children if the assistants change frequently.

Siblings

Parents of multiples (twins, triplets, etc.) need to look at schools with a slightly different perspective. You need to find a school that recognizes the unique relationship that twins and other multiples share, while encouraging the individual strengths of each child. Preschool is generally not a good time to separate the multiples into different classes. You will need, however, an experienced teacher who will encourage the siblings to reach out to other children.

Ask the director about the school's experience with multiples. Do the teachers understand the emotional bond twins often share? twinspeak? One preschool celebrated a year of multiple blessings when the three-year-old class, with 14 children, had three sets of twins! There had been some concern, among the parents of the other students, that the classroom dynamics might be affected. Through the skillfull practice of a team of experienced teachers, it was a successful year for all the students.

Special Needs

If your child has been identified with a physical, intellectual, or emotional disability, you will need to make a decision about the kind of preschool that is right for him. Sometimes a disability is not diagnosed until the child is in preschool and an experienced teacher points out the problem to the parents. It is estimated that between 10 percent and 20 percent of all children may be considered to have special needs.

Children at risk enjoy long-term benefits from attending the proper preschool coupled with early intervention that includes diagnosis and appropriate support. Studies have shown that those children who receive the appropriate therapy and attend a good preschool program are more likely to graduate from high school and less likely to repeat a grade; they may also need fewer special services later in school. Furthermore, early intervention is helpful for families as well. They feel less isolation and less stress because their child is receiving help.

Depending on the severity of the disability, the school curriculum, the teachers and preschool administration, and your own comfort level, you may decide that a mainstream public or private preschool is the right place for your child. This is a decision that must be a collaborative effort made in consultation with the preschool, your child's doctors, perhaps a preschool educational psychologist, and drawing upon your own parental sense of who your child is and what is best for him.

Mainstreaming Your Child

The advantages of enrolling your special needs child in a mainstream public or private preschool are:

1. Your child will have better role models if he is placed in a regular classroom. If he is exclusively with children with disabilities he may not be exposed to age-appropriate behaviors.
2. The expectations for your child may be more demanding and children often attempt to meet the level of expectation. For example, in a regular classroom where a child hears other

children speaking, a child with a lag in speech development may be more likely to try to use language to communicate.

3. Being in a regular class environment may ease acceptance of a child with a disability. Peers, parents, and the community will see that a disabled child can function in a regular class-room.

4. Having a child with special needs in the class is helpful for the development of all children. Children learn at an early age that disabilities need not affect friendship or an individual's abilities to function in a community.

DISADVANTAGES

The disadvantages of mainstreaming your special needs child are:

1. It may be more difficult to coordinate treatment schedule. An intensive therapy program may overlap regular school hours or may be too demanding.

2. A specialized preschool program may offer a community of support for both the child and her family.

3. A regular preschool program may not meet your child's needs; the teachers may not be experienced to handle your situation; the school may not have a *can do* attitude toward making it work for your child.

Your school district may provide a public preschool program for children with special needs that includes therapy. Public Law 94-142, the Education for All Handicapped Children Act, requires that each state identify, screen, evaluate, and provide appropriate educational services for all children with physical, mental, or emotional handicaps beginning in kindergarten. Your school district may offer preschool programs for at-risk children under the federally funded Chapter 1 Program for low-income families. If your school district chooses to participate, you may qualify for these programs even if your income exceeds the limits. Check with your school board and special education department to see if you meet eligibility requirements.

THE BEST OF BOTH WORLDS

Depending upon the severity of your child's disability, you may be able to take advantage of both a mainstream classroom and a special needs program. One family enrolled their daughter, who had a developmental delay in speech, in a mainstream nursery school in the morning and a public pre-K program geared for learning disabled children in the afternoon. The child benefited from participating in both programs and received the early intervention therapy she needed.

The decision to enroll in both programs needs to be made in consultation with the directors of both programs, as well as the appropriate therapists. A dual program can be a heavy load for a young child to carry, but if successful, will be a great service to the child. Success depends upon the commitment of the family and both schools to make this type of dual program work.

You may qualify for an aide to accompany your child to a mainstream preschool. One Downs syndrome child attended the regular four-year-old class in her local preschool, but was assisted by a state-funded aide. The classroom teachers were excellent, but all agree that having the extra pair of hands in the classroom were essential to making the situation work for both the child and the rest of the students.

Comprehensive Schools (Preschool through 12th grade)

Some families choose an ongoing school for their child. The youngster is enrolled in preschool and remains in the same school through high-school graduation. The advantages of choosing this type of school include:

✎ **Educational continuity** The child becomes accustomed to the school and the school gets to know the child and family over a period of years.

✎ **Logistics** It may be easier to have all the children in the family in one location.

✎ **Role models** The older students in the school serve as role models, and the interaction between the grades can be good for all children.

There are also some disadvantages to this type of school situation.

✎ A preschool that ends at age five, focuses on that age group and those activities, whereas an educational institution that houses a preschool-12-grade program may have competing pressures.

✎ It's difficult to make long-term academic decisions about your child when he is only two years old. If you choose just a preschool, you will have the opportunity to rethink educational settings at kindergarten age.

✎ The physical setting in a preschool may be better suited to young children.

✎ In a preschool setting, the "graduate" (four- or five-year-old) can feel like the oldest, and serve as a role model. In a preschool-12 institution, the student has to wait a very long time to be the oldest in the school.

✎ The child may perceive the preschool-12 school as an institution that is designed for how he will be, not how he is.

Head Start

As described by the U.S. government, "the overall goal of Head Start is to bring about a greater degree of social competence in children of low-income families. By social competence is meant the child's everyday effectiveness in dealing with both the present environment and later responsibilities in school and life." (U.S. Department of Health and Human Services, 1984).

One of the best-known components of Head Start is the free (federally funded) preschool education program, which serves disadvantaged children and their families. More than 740,000 youngsters and their families are served each year. There are over 1,400 community-based programs across the country. Ten percent of the enrollment is reserved for children with disabilities. Nearly 70 percent of the families in Head Start programs have incomes of less than $9,000 per year, and over 80 percent have yearly incomes of less than $12,000.

Now over 30 years old, Head Start programs also include health, education, parent involvement, and social services. They are designed to meet the needs of the child in the context of the family. Parents are encouraged to volunteer in the classroom, participate in home visits by the teacher at least twice a year, attend parent education classes, enroll in job training programs, literacy programs, or adult education programs, as well as participate on policy-making bodies and the state, regional, or national Head Start programs.

For more information on Head Start programs in your area, contact your local board of education or local social service agencies.

What Do You Hope Your Child Learns in Preschool?

No matter what program you choose for your child, you would hope that when she "graduates" from preschool your child will have gained these skills:

1. She is able to get along and function in a group.
2. She is able to share.
3. She knows that different behaviors are appropriate at different times and places.
4. She has a willingness to listen and pay attention.
5. She is able to focus on a task and complete it.
6. She can set goals and achieve them.

Any program you choose should help your child develop a positive attitude about herself. This solid, positive sense of self is critical in order to learn. The school should build a youngster's self-esteem by giving her experiences that challenge her, not overwhelm or frustrate her.

Questions and Answers

Q: I would prefer to enroll my daughter in a Montessori pre-school, but there aren't any in my area. What should I do?

A: You would be wise to look for the best preschool program in your area, even if it is not a Montessori-affiliated program. You could then incorporate Montessori techniques at home. *Teaching Montessori in the Home* by Elizabeth Hainstock provides parents with activities that can be done with their child at home to foster the Montessori method of learning. While the school materials are expensive and designed for continual use by hundreds of students, you can develop similar materials at home. The emphasis on practical living, one of the core components of the Montessori program, is certainly easy to incorporate into your family life. For example, encourage your child to pour her own juice by providing her with a small pitcher, placed on an accessible lower shelf in the refrigerator.

Q: I am Jewish and my husband is Catholic. We have decided to expose our son to the customs and traditions of both religions. Will it be confusing if we send him to a preschool affiliated with the Reform Jewish movement?

A: Children adjust easily to situations where the grown-ups have their best interests at heart. A good preschool program is sensitive to a child's needs and questions. But it's very important to discuss this issue with the director of the school before you enroll your son. It's quite likely that she has dealt with this issue before. It's also helpful to know what is the temple's policy on interfaith families. Is it a welcoming atmosphere?

You and your husband need to be comfortable with the school policy before your child enters the program. Obviously you should not expect the school to celebrate Christmas or any other non-Jewish holiday. On the other hand, it would be unfair to your son if the school was unprepared to deal with his understandable comments and excitement about the holidays he is celebrating at home. Get specific in your discussion. Describe a holiday scenario, for example: "My child wants to talk about Santa Claus, and then ask the director how the teachers would handle the situation. You may decide that placing your child in a Jewish preschool program will strengthen his understanding of the religion. Consider if your husband will be comfortable with this choice. This can work, but only if all the parties are committed to making it work.

Q: **My daughter has diabetes. She takes insulin and her diet is strictly controlled. Do we need to tell the preschool before we enroll her since we don't want her singled out as anyone special? We are determined to make her childhood as normal as possible.**

A: It's important to discuss your child's medical situation with the director before you enroll her in class. If you don't feel that you are getting answers that clearly indicate a commitment to as normal a preschool experience as possible, or that your child will somehow be made to feel different than the other children, or that the staff feels unable to cope with a child who has a chronic medical condition, then you want to look for another program. There is no reason why a school shouldn't be able to accommodate your child's needs. Of course, you need to be clear with the preschool about any dietary restrictions your daughter has, but this is not unusual. Many children have milk intolerance or wheat allergies, and the school adjusts its snack for that child.

As for the children in the class, kids are curious, but remarkably tolerant about differences. A clear explanation to the class, "Mary has diabetes and can't eat doughnuts so she is going to have crackers today," generally satisfies children. You want your own child to become comfortable explaining her medical needs to others since that will help her become responsible for her health—an important step in building her self-esteem. You'll want to discuss her dietary needs with the parents of any classmates when your daughter has a play date at another child's home. Offer to send a snack for both children.

Q: **I've been looking at two preschools in our area. One is more modern and even has several computers for each classroom. The other is somewhat old fashioned with no**

computers, although the kids seemed to be having a good time, and I did like the teachers. How important is computer literacy at this point? Will it give my kid an "edge" in starting school?

A: We know that computers will play an important role in your child's future, but they are not important in a preschool curriculum. Children at this age need hands-on activities that involve all their senses and an environment that encourages them to explore and discover the world surrounding them. While computers can be fun and educational for preschoolers, they shouldn't be the deciding factor in choosing a program. You were right to concentrate on looking at the children and the classroom teachers. There will be plenty of time for your child to become computer literate—and, of course, if you have a home computer, there are many fine programs that are geared for this age group.

2

THE ABC'S OF CHOOSING A PRESCHOOL

Choosing the right preschool for your child requires you to visit, observe, and evaluate what you see *and what you don't see*. Some of what you observe is quantifiable: the educational qualifications of the staff; whether or not the school is accredited; the age and condition of the playground equipment; the availability of a gym for indoor days; enrichment programs that are offered. And some of the evaluation will be on a *gut level*, your own best instincts about the people you meet, the school community, and how your child *and you* will fit in.

How to Start?

Even if you have already decided that you want a Montessori program or a religiously affiliated preschool, you would be wise to start with an open mind. You won't know if your program in theory is the best program in reality. How the theories are executed is more important than what is written down on a mission statement. So while you may choose to look for a specific program, keep your ears and mind open to other possibilities. Here are some ways to find schools in your area.

✎ Of course, **word of mouth** is generally the best resource. Other families in your community may recommend or criticize a local preschool. Consider the source and listen carefully to the criticisms. The problems reported may not be an issue for you or may reflect different child-rearing practices or expectations.

✎ Check your **church or synagogue**. Many religious institutions either sponsor a preschool or rent space to a program.

✎ The local **YMCA or YMHA** may also house preschool programs.

✎ Your **pediatrician** is another good resource for local programs.

✎ Call your **local school board** to find out about any public pre-K programs.

✎ Go **on-line** and check with parenting forums. Many parents post queries about their specific geographic area on bulletin boards and get responses from other local preschool parents. (See appendix for on-line parenting resources.)

✎ Check the **Yellow Pages** of your local directory under preschools, nursery schools, day care.

What's the Right Age to Begin Preschool?

Just 20 years ago, most preschool programs were for three- and four-year-olds. Now the majority have classes for two-year-olds, and some for even younger. Certainly, day-care centers offer developmentally appropriate programs for children under two.

Should you enroll your two-year-old in school or wait an extra year or even two? That's a parental decision that you will make based on what's available and what works best for you and your child.

One alternative is the "Mommy and Me" program. Although the title is somewhat antiquated, since it's frequently populated by caregivers and their charges (and some dads and their offspring), nonetheless, it may be a good introduction to preschool. In these programs, a parent or caregiver stays with the child during the program. Sometimes, the parents/caregivers separate from the children during part of the class for support group discussions while the children play with a teacher. You'll want to know what proportion of the class is brought to school with a caregiver and how many are accompanied by a parent. You don't want your child to be the "only" of either one. And if you are looking to find other parents of preschoolers, you'll want to know if this is a good resource.

Or you may choose a regular class program for your two-year-old. Some schools have two-day, three-day, even five-day a week programs for two-year-olds. Assuming they are developmentally appropriate, you may choose to enroll your child. One concern, however, if you opt for a five-day a week program, is whether the school curriculum changes appropriately for three-year-olds and then fours. You don't want you child to get bored if the program remains essentially the same for the twos and threes. That doesn't mean that they don't cover many of the same topics. It's how they approach the subjects that's important.

When looking at a two-year-old program, keep in mind:

✎ whether your two-year-old will have the opportunity to be with other children or does he already have plenty of occasions to be around other kids (story hours, gym programs, play groups);

✎ whether you want some time away from your child knowing she is in a safe environment (and that is a natural and understandable parental need);

✎ whether the program is geared to the developmental level of a two-year-old with no emphasis on academics and much stress on play.

Depending on your answers, then enrolling your child in a preschool program for two-year-olds may be right for your family.

But keep in mind, as the next section describes, you should begin your search a year before you plan to enroll your child. That means you will be making this decision when your youngster is probably just beginning to walk. Remember that your child will be making enormous strides in language, physical, intellectual, and social development between his first and second birthdays. The program you select should reflect where he will be at that time, not his current level.

When to Start the Search?

You should start your search *at least a full year* before you plan to enroll your child. It may be hard to imagine, as you look at a classroom full of children, that your baby or toddler will ever be ready for school. Some parents worry that their child may change dramatically in 12 months and the choice they make today won't be right a year later. Others are concerned that the teacher they observe and think is just perfect won't be there next year.

Although these worries are legitimate, it is reassuring to know that while your child will undoubtedly mature over a year, you are looking, in the broad sense, for a basic philosophical match between your approach to kids and the school's program; for a caring, creative staff who clearly enjoy working with young children; for a safe, nurturing environment. Therefore, if it's a well-run program, in a clean, safe environment, with a caring, professional staff, then it will still be a good match a year later, even though your child is very different than the toddler of 12 months earlier, and even if the teacher you adore has left.

The search process helps you to focus on what you believe is important in a preschool program. It allows you time to see how different preschools handle similar problems. It permits you to picture yourself within a school community. And allowing yourself enough time to search gives you the widest number of choices. Many quality programs, especially in urban areas, fill up early. It's not unusual for a preschool to close its enrollment nine months or more before the opening of school. Some schools take names of prospective students at birth! Check out your community to see what is the pattern for the schools in your area.

Sometimes you don't have the luxury of time. One single working mother was forced to choose a school midyear when her baby-sitter developed health problems. After an intense two-week search, she found three local schools that she liked and each one had an opening.

Although your options may be limited, **never compromise on safety.** If you feel you have had to settle for a safe but less than perfect program, consider enrolling your child and then taking the time to find a preschool for the following year that better suits your needs.

Most schools require a nonrefundable deposit when you decide to enroll your child. You will want to be sure of your decision before you write the check!

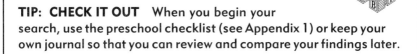

TIP: CHECK IT OUT When you begin your search, use the preschool checklist (see Appendix 1) or keep your own journal so that you can review and compare your findings later.

Scheduling the First Visit

The first visit to a preschool should be *without* your child. It's a scouting mission. You need time to observe and ask questions without distraction. It also can be confusing for your young child who may be developmentally unready to fit into a classroom situation; or your child may want to settle down and play with the toys just when you are ready to move on to another site within the school; or your little one may be frightened or overwhelmed by the activities or noise in the classroom and cling to you. You may later want to visit a number of schools with your child, but this first visit should be for adults only.

Call for an appointment to visit. It's unfair to expect the staff to show you the school if you stop by unexpectedly. Try to be as flexible as possible in making the appointment. Some schools prefer to offer group meetings for parents of prospective students. The staff is trying to minimize class disruptions.

Let Your Fingers Do the Walking

You can get the answers to many of your basic questions during the first phone call.

1. What is the ratio of adults to children?
Preschoolers need a lot of one-on-one attention. Look for a preschool class that has the recommended number of adults per child and a class size that is small enough. You need that level of coverage to ensure a high quality and safe program. The National Association for the Education of Young Children (NAEYC) is the nation's largest membership organization of early childhood professionals and

others dedicated to improving the quality of services for young children and their families. NAEYC recommendations are:

Age	Adults to Children Ratio	Class Size
2 year olds	1 adult per 7 children	No more than 14
3 year olds	1 adult per 7 children	No more than 14
4 year olds	1 adult per 10 children	No more than 20
5 year olds	1 adult per 10 children	No more than 20

2. What are the educational credentials of the staff?

The NAEYC recommends that at least one staff member in the school holds an undergraduate degree in early childhood education. It's not that an experienced teacher can't be effective without a degree. But you want a school that keeps up with the latest research in the field, that sees early childhood education as a career, and that provides opportunities for the staff for professional development.

3. Is the school accredited? Is it licensed by all appropriate state and local authorities?

Not all schools will seek accreditation from a national organization, but it is a good indication of a program's commitment to high standards if it has undergone the process. Smaller schools, with less than 60 students, may find the process too lengthy and involved and choose not to participate.

Two groups, The National Academy of Early Childhood Programs, a NAEYC division, and the National Association of Independent Schools (NAIS) offer national accreditation. Both require schools to meet national standards in curriculum; staff-child and staff-parent interaction; staff qualifications and development; administration; staffing; physical environment; health and safety; nutrition and food service.

> **TIP:** Allow at least an hour for each preschool. This will give you time to see the children move between several activities. You also want to talk to the school director for at least 15 minutes.

Licensing by appropriate state and local authorities is an absolute requirement. Check with your local health department to see if the schools you are visiting are licensed. It is no guarantee of excellence, but it at least insures compliance with minimum health and safety requirements

4. Are there any openings in the program for the upcoming school year?

If the classes are already filled a year in advance, you may choose not to visit the school, even if its reputation is excellent. If the classes are already filled for the following year, ask if you may put your child on the waiting list in case an opening arises. It still may be worth a visit to see the program for a number of reasons.

✎ You may want to see a good program as a point of comparison.
✎ You may want to consider this program as an alternative for another year (or for a younger child).
✎ Often an opening will arise before school starts (families move, the parents decide to make other plans).

5. Brochures

Ask if the school has any brochures or pamphlets describing the program. If so, ask to have them mailed to you so you can review them before your visit. You will want to see if reality matches the description. You may discover that the program emphasizes activities that are of no interest to you. For example, the brochure may highlight school computers. This may signal that the emphasis is more on academics and less on socialization. Computers are wonderful, and can be terrific learning tools, but in preschool the emphasis should be on the basics: learning to share, cooperate, explore the world, using the five senses to grow intellectually, emotionally, and physically.

Location

Where the school is located may be one of the most important factors in your decision. Some parents prefer that the school is a community-based program; others want the school to be within a short walk or car ride; and some want the program near their place of work rather than near home. There are advantages and disadvantages with any of the choices.

Near Home A school that is within a short walk or car ride to your home generally means less rushing in the morning. If you need only allow 10 minutes to get to school, your preschooler can experiment dressing herself; dawdling can be built into the schedule. Carpooling may be easier to arrange and play dates are likely to be more convenient. Your child may make friends with youngsters who will go on to kindergarten with her. Some working parents need a local preschool because their child-care help doesn't have a car and must walk the child to school (or take local transportation). A school close to home also gives parents the opportunity to find a local community of adult friendships with parents of other young children.

Near Work Some parents choose a school near their jobs in order to be close in case of an emergency. They also enjoy the additional time they can spend with their child during the commute. This alternative works best if after-school child care is also nearby.

Near Child Care You may prefer to choose a school that is located conveniently for your baby-sitter. One family opted to put their son in the church-based preschool near their sitter. The woman watched several children in her home and preferred that her charges all attended the same preschool so she could easily pick them up at the same time.

But some parents are so committed to a certain program that they are willing to go outside of their community or drive a distance in order to participate. It may be worth it but keep in mind that car pools and play dates may be more difficult to arrange.

The Environment: Indoors

Kids need room to play. The NAEYC recommends **a minimum of 35 square feet of indoor usable playroom floor space per child.** You won't need to carry a yardstick to get the exact room measurements. Your eyes will tell you at a glance:

✎ whether the children seem crowded in the classroom;
✎ whether there is adequate room to move around (for example, can the children take their instruments and march around the room or move creatively to music?);
✎ whether the classroom can comfortably house a variety of activity centers;
✎ whether there is enough space for children to work both individually and in groups.

The Classroom

The basics: Is the classroom

✎ clean?
✎ well organized?
✎ well maintained?
✎ recently painted? is there any peeling paint?
✎ well ventilated? is the room damp or musty?
✎ attractively decorated? are the decorations appropriate for preschoolers?
✎ well lit? are electrical cords and plugs safely covered?
✎ safe? are toxic materials locked away?
✎ child oriented? are there individual cubbies for personal belongings (a change of clothes, art projects to go home) and individual hooks for coats?

The Furniture

✎ well maintained?
✎ sturdy?
✎ appropriately sized for preschoolers?
✎ Are there enough chairs for all the children in the class? tables for snacks and art projects?

Classroom Organization

Most classrooms are organized into several different activity centers. Look for:

An art area that includes easels for painting, drop cloths/newspapers for the floor, smocks or old shirts (each student may supply her own). Play-Doh/clay is a preschool staple and excellent for improving small-motor skills (besides being fun!).

There should be plentiful creative art supplies, perhaps available in another part of the room, including markers, pens, crayons, and paint brushes.

Other art basics are: blunt safety scissors (and some for left-handed preschoolers as well), glue sticks, liquid white glue, blank white paper, and colored construction paper. Look for a bin of household recyclables that can be used for projects including empty coffee cans, cereal boxes, juices cans, plastic soda bottles, egg cartons, foam meat trays, etc.

Creative art corners will include materials from nature such as pine cones and shells, as well as: felt and material scraps; ribbon; glitter, beads, sequins; scraps of well-sanded wood; empty thread spools; hole punch; yarn; pipe cleaners; paper doilies; feathers; buttons; dried pasta; old magazines, greeting cards, picture postcards.

A book corner that is inviting, perhaps carpeted, with floor pillows. It should be a place where a child can comfortably sit with a book and read. The books should be attractively displayed and easily accessible by children for browsing/reading. There should be a combination of fiction and nonfiction books available. Look for colorful picture books, some with little or no text, as well as books with more challenging levels of reading. There should be a range of books in each classroom so that children at all levels of development can find something to "read" (whether or not they are actually reading the words).

A block corner that is well equipped and organized. Children love to play with blocks. These simple toys unleash their imaginations and creativity. Look for smooth wooden blocks in a variety of shapes,

---

TIP: Look for handheld writing and art tools with fat shafts. These are easier for preschoolers to grasp and manipulate.

---

stacked on low shelves. Nearby should be empty floor space for building.

Tables and chairs with enough child-sized chairs and tables for every child to be able to sit and draw, create, or have snacks/lunch. Again the emphasis is on sturdy, smooth, well-maintained furniture that is appropriately sized for young children.

A housekeeping area that is furnished with a play stove, refrigerator, sink, pots and pans, dishes, plastic foods, even perhaps a small table and chairs for tea parties or to act as a grocery store checkout counter. This is a place where young children can model adult roles. Nearby may be a dress-up box with plenty of costumes, hats, shoes, and accessories to complete the fantasy play. (Pure Montessori schools may not have this activity area.)

A water/sand table Not all schools will have this equipment, but it is a definite plus and a good sign of a child-oriented program. A water table (a tub built into a sturdy wooden frame), which can alternatively be filled with sand, is a great hands-on piece of equipment. Children love water, and a water table gives them an opportunity to wash toys, pour from one container to another, or practice measuring. It's great for small-motor control—and great fun!

A science/nature area Are there plants, animals, or other natural science objects in the room? Young children enjoy and learn when they care for animals and observe nature.

Nap or rest-time equipment If this is a full-day program, then there should be an area and equipment, mats or fold-up cots, on which young children can take a rest during the extended afternoon. While not all youngsters will actually sleep, a specific quiet time for rest is essential.

Equipment/toys

Preschool toys and equipment are generally not what you buy for your child at home. Nor are they the trendy toys that are advertised on television. Instead they are the classics, like puzzles, wooden blocks, Legos, trucks, sewing cards, sorters, the kinds of toys that children have played with for generations. They are open-ended with no "right way" to play with them. A child can use the blocks to build a castle, a bed, a spaceship, or even pretend that individual blocks are people.

✎ Are the toys on low shelves where a child can readily get to them? The best equipment and toys are worthless if a child can't easily use them. You want to look at the quality and variety of toys and equipment, but you also want to know if children can reach them, take them out to play and then be able to put them away at clean-up time.

✎ Are the toys well organized so that similar toys are grouped together?

✎ Are the toys age appropriate and sufficient in quantity for the number of children in the class? This doesn't necessarily mean duplicates, but enough alternatives so that a child can always find an interesting activity.

✎ Are there puzzles, construction sets, blocks, and manipulative items? Are there simple board games such as lotto or Candy Land?

Art Projects

The children's art that decorates the walls in the classroom give a remarkably clear insight into the school's general approach to preschoolers. Is the school interested in the product or the process?

One mother was appalled when she saw a teacher adding cotton balls to a snowman project that a young child had just completed. The teacher thought the snowman "didn't look full enough."

Is the art individualistic or cookie-cutter duplicates? It's fine to have some class projects that use similar materials, for example, decorating a frame with a variety of materials from nature. But each child should be able to decide which and how much of the materials she chooses to use.

Bathrooms/Diaper-Changing Area

Young children need easy, quick access to bathrooms. Self-control at this age is limited, even for those who are already toilet trained.

✎ Are the bathrooms readily accessible to the classroom? Ideally, there would be a bathroom directly off each classroom. If not, do young children have to walk through hallways to get to the bathrooms? Are they accompanied by an adult? What happens if a child needs help?

✎ Are the fixtures appropriately sized for young children? Are there enough stalls?

✎ **Is the hot water temperature no more than 110 degrees** Fahrenheit to avoid scalding? Some schools turn off the hot-water tap in the children's bathrooms.

✎ For those children not yet toilet trained, is there a specific area for changing diapers? Is the changing table clean and sturdy? Are there rubber gloves available for staff to wear when changing diapers? Is there running water nearby so that the staff can wash their hands after a diaper change? Is the diaper pail covered and changed regularly?

Indoor Gym

Beyond the classroom, but still indoors, what space is available for play on inclement days? While most preschools try to include time each day to take the youngsters outdoors (except under the most dire weather conditions), there should be a plan for indoor play.

✎ Does the school have access to a gym?

✎ Alternatively, some schools use hallways, meeting rooms, or the basement for large-group indoor play. Are these areas large enough to accommodate riding vehicles and indoor climbing structures? Could children play with a ball?

✎ Whatever the area chosen, is it well maintained, well lit, and well ventilated? Is there a damp, musty odor if it is in the basement?

The Environment: Outdoors

The area surrounding the preschool also needs to be safe and well supervised. During arrival and pickup, the potential for danger is great because of the mix of young children and traffic. Furthermore, the outdoor play area is an integral part of any preschool curriculum. It should be examined with a critical eye.

Arrival/Dismissal

What are the arrival/dismissal plans for the school? Children should be safely and properly supervised by the staff during drop off and pickup. There are many ways to handle these potentially dangerous situations. Some schools insist that all cars park in a lot away from the school and parents/caregivers then walk over and pick up their child/car pool. Others have a drive-through procedure where the cars line up and then each child (and her car pool mates) is placed into the car by the staff.

If the school is located in an urban area where children walk to school or use public transportation, what are the strategies for ensuring a safe transference from caregiver to staff, and then the reverse at the end of the day? **Does the school's plan seem safe and appropriate for its location?**

Other points to consider:

✎ Are parking lots well maintained and well lit?

✎ If there is private bus service, how do the children get to the buses? Does a staff member accompany them on the bus? Are the buses well maintained with a safety belt for each child (or car seat if appropriate)? Who buckles in each child?

School Security

While the school should have an open-door policy for parents that permits you to visit and, when appropriate, participate, the school should also have a clear procedure to screen visitors and keep out strangers. Basic safety precautions should also be clearly in evidence.

✎ Do all visitors have to check in at the main office and wear an identifying badge?

✎ Are outer doors locked and a procedure in place to admit/screen visitors?

✎ Are there crash bars (rather than door knobs) on all outside doors so that a youngster can easily exit in an emergency?

✎ Are there working fire alarms and fire extinguishers in each classroom/hallway and emergency lights? Is there a posted emergency exit plan?

> **TIP:** Never double-park or leave your car idling or in gear while you go inside to pick up.

✎ Does the school hold frequent fire drills with the children?

✎ Can all classrooms be easily evacuated—even those above the first floor?

The Outdoor Playground

Young children need to run and climb. Part of every preschool day should include an opportunity for them to exercise their large-motor muscles. A good preschool should either have their own appropriately sized playground, or easy access to one. One church-based program used the kindergarten playground of the public school located across the street from them.

Here's what to look for:

✎ The NAEYC recommends playgrounds provide at least 75 square feet per child.

✎ The playground should be fenced.

✎ The surface under the equipment should be impact absorbing. Look for a play area that is built over *properly maintained* loose-filled material such as wood mulch, pea gravel, or sand. In order to be impact absorbing, the materials should be at least 9 to 12 inches deep (so these materials need to be replenished over time). Synthetic, foamlike tiles or rubber mats made especially for playground use are also safe.

✎ The equipment should be scaled for young children. Equipment should be no more than 5 feet high. There should be a protective surface below and a 6- to 8-foot perimeter surrounding the equipment so that a child can descend safely without falling onto another child or structure. Any platform or walkway more than 20 inches above the ground should have guardrails or protective barriers.

✎ The equipment should be well maintained. Run your fingers over wooden climbing structures and check for splinters and look for loose screws.

✎ If there are riding toys, are they appropriately sized? Is there space to ride? Does the school own enough riding toys (although not necessarily one per child) so that several children can enjoy them without waiting too long for a turn?

✎ Is the sandbox covered after use to avoid animal droppings?

✎ Are there bathrooms nearby? Who accompanies the child to the bathroom?

The Staff

The school staff, which includes the director, teachers, aides, and any specialists that are brought in, is probably the single most important component of a good preschool program. All the fancy equipment, educational toys, and impressive campus features can't make up for a bad teacher. You can check credentials, experience, and college degrees, *and you should*, but much of what you must decide about a teacher is on a *gut level*. Ideally you will walk out of a preschool visit impressed with the professional, caring approach of the staff.

Staff turnover Generally it's a positive sign if the rate of turnover is low. On the other hand, salaries for early childhood education workers are notoriously low and professionals often must seek more remunerative jobs.

1. How many of the staff have been there for at least five years?
2. How long has the director been in that position? If she is new, how long was the previous director in place?
3. Who makes the hiring/firing decisions, the school director or the school board (generally a group of parents and sometimes representatives from the affiliated house of worship or the community)?

Staff Development Does the staff meet on a regular basis to plan and evaluate the program? Does the director insist upon, and make time for, staff development? Does she build into the schedule opportunities for the staff to attend conferences and meetings on early childhood development?

Staff Credentials   Ask the director about the education and experience of her staff. Does she check references? Does she call local law enforcement authorities for a security check on all new hires.

Medical Emergencies   Who is responsible for handling medical emergencies—the director or classroom teachers?

1. Is anyone on the staff trained in CPR?
2. Is there a basic first-aid kit in every classroom?
3. Are teachers trained to handle minor medical emergencies (e.g., bumps, bruises, scrapes, and cuts)?
4. What is the plan for major medical emergencies (e.g., serious falls, convulsions)?
5. What are the school rules for keeping a sick child home? For example, while everyone would agree that a child with a temperature does not belong in school, what about runny noses?
6. If food is regularly prepared on the premises (for example, a hot-lunch program), where is the kitchen? Are stoves out of the traffic pattern of young children? Is the kitchen supervised by the local health department?

The Director

The director of the preschool program sets the tone for the school. In addition to being responsible for a myriad of administrative details, generally she hires the teaching staff. The director should believe in and be able to articulate the school's educational philosophy. When necessary she serves as a buffer between parents and staff, and should be a resource for the entire school community.

The director should have strong educational and professional credentials, preferably a master's degree in early childhood education, and should have been a classroom teacher herself. In some smaller schools, the director also teaches in the program. The advantages of having a director with no classroom responsibilities are that it frees her to supervise the staff, as well as act as a roving consultant in the different classrooms. It also makes her more available to parents and able to handle emergencies.

✎ The director should be articulate, sensitive, open, and warm to adults and children, as she will have to deal with both.

✎ She should be well organized because much of her job is in the details.

The Classroom Teachers

Preschool teachers come in all shapes and sizes. They are not all clones of Mary Poppins—nor do you want them to be. You might not necessarily choose one as your best friend. In fact, you may not have much in common with your child's preschool teacher **except a mutual commitment to ensuring the best for your child's first school experience.**

Teachers come into the classroom with different styles and with different personalities, *but it should be readily apparent that they like what they do.* Preschool teaching is a wonderfully rewarding, underpaid, underappreciated profession. You have to be doing it for love because you couldn't be doing it for the money. On the other hand, you want to choose a program that values teachers and pays enough to attract a highly qualified staff.

✎ **Education** Ideally, the preschool teacher will have a degree in early childhood education. If she does not have a college- or graduate-level degree in a related field, she should have a basic understanding of the developmental patterns of young children and a commitment to a program that meets those needs.

✎ **Experience** Equally important, if not more so, than an early childhood education degree, is practical work experience in a preschool classroom. *Been there, seen that* is invaluable when working with young children. The perspective you gain after working in the field for several years eases many of the day-to-day classroom crises. It is also incredibly reassuring to parents if a teacher, based on her years of experience, can help put a troublesome situation in perspective.

✎ **Personality** This is key to a teacher's effectiveness. Of course, there should be an underlying warmth and friendliness in her approach. But don't be limited into thinking that there is only one kind of personality that fits the ideal preschool teacher.

Children respond positively to a variety of personalities and styles. A nursery-school teacher doesn't necessarily have to be an affectionate, grandmotherly type to be effective.

One superb preschool teacher was an older woman, reserved, and British. She had a no-nonsense approach, but children adored her because she clearly adored them. She loved nature and her room was filled with a variety of objects that young children could explore, such as a giant sunflower that children could look at under a microscope that she had brought into her classroom. On the one hand she insisted on proper manners at the snack table, including napkins on each child's lap; she didn't brook pushing and shoving in line; and expected—and got—courteous behavior from rowdy four-year-olds. But she *also listened* when her students talked to her; laughed when they told a "knock-knock" joke for the 50th time; and helped build a snowman with her students after the first snowfall. Without question she enjoyed four-year-olds—and they knew it.

But while it is essential that the preschool teacher have a genuine rapport with her students, she should also be able to relate well to adults. This is a partnership that is about to be developed. *Are you comfortable with this teacher?* Can you see yourself talking to her, confiding in her, respecting her opinion (although not necessarily always agreeing with it)?

Humor As any parent knows, a sense of humor is essential for raising children. To survive with sanity intact, adults need to be able to laugh at many of the trials of life with young children. At the same time, one of the most endearing qualities of a preschooler is his developing sense of humor. It's much more than just bathroom jokes (although there are probably too many of those!). Preschool teachers will encourage a child's sense of humor by reading books with funny twists of story line, singing silly songs ("I Know an Old Lady Who Swallowed a Fly"), and inviting youngsters to see the funny side to a potential problem. A good sense of humor is crucial in a preschool teacher.

Special talents This is a bonus. Does the teacher have any special talents that she can share with her students, such as playing the guitar?

45

✔CHECK IT OUT

When you observe the teacher in the classroom, you'll want to notice:

1. How does the teacher handle transitions? Many youngsters have trouble moving from one activity to another—from art project to story time; from free play to clean up. How well a teacher can handle a child's natural reluctance to move on from a fun activity is a good barometer of how she handles difficult situations.

2. Does the teacher often stoop down to talk at eye level with her students? When an adult gets down to a child's level it shows a basic respect and interest.

3. Does the teacher frequently raise her voice, either in anger or to get the children's attention? If a teacher has to raise her voice often it may mean that she doesn't have control of her class. Teachers will sometimes use silent signals, such as flicking the lights off and on, to grab the attention of the class.

4. Does she really listen to her students? Of course, every parent has at one time listened with half an ear while finishing another project, but for the most part, *does the teacher seem to be paying attention as a child talks to her?*

5. Is the teacher articulate? Children model language and you want a teacher who uses correct grammar and speaks clearly. Does she use open-ended questions with the children so that they will stretch their use of language?

6. Are the rules of the classroom clear? How does the teacher handle aggression among the children? How does she handle a situation calling for discipline? Does she use time-outs? Are they appropriate in length? You should never see any name-calling or belittling by either teachers or children.

TIP: Don't underestimate your instincts. You will know a good preschool teacher with *genuine* warmth and friendliness when you meet her.

TIP: The general rule of thumb is one minute of time-out per year of age, (that is, a three-minute time-out is appropriate for a three-year-old).

7. How do students address the teacher? Do they use the staff's first names or address them more formally, for example, Ms. Smith and Mrs. Jones? Actually, it doesn't matter whether it's formal or informal. What is important is how relaxed and comfortable are the teachers with young children.

Discipline

Like a good football team, the best offense is a good defense. The best discipline policies are when the rules are clear, developmentally appropriate, and never belittle or emotionally (or physically) abuse a child.

In preschools, a good teacher heads off potential problems, keeping an eye on situations that may possibly be heading for danger. For example, two children begin to squabble over a toy.

✎ A teacher first will try to help the two youngsters problem solve the conflict themselves. She'll encourage them to use their words, not their hands. She'll ask: "How can the two of you share the tricycle?"

✎ She might pose possible resolutions: "Jamie can ride the tricycle and Steve will be the traffic officer, and then you can switch."

✎ Or if necessary she may impose a solution: "Jamie can ride the tricycle until the timer rings, and then it is Steve's turn."

A good preschool teacher will also distract a youngster she sees heading down a road she knows is trouble. She might suggest to a youngster who is losing self-control while playing in the water table that he switch over to building with clay or look at a book for a change. It's not punitive, but rather an attempt to get the youngster to calm down and regain control.

A preschool teacher also knows what is developmentally appropriate for young children. She doesn't put her charges in situations where they are bound to fail. For example, knowing youngsters have difficulty waiting long for a turn, a teacher will have inviting alternative activities available when the students have to share a popular toy.

Teachers should also describe the behavior they want in positive terms rather than negative ones. They might say: "Please put newspapers down on the floor before painting," rather than "You're so messy when you paint."

When observing a preschool class, you should see teachers giving frequent, positive reinforcement for good behavior rather than constant struggling to maintain control of the class.

Gender Equity in the Classroom

When you observe the classroom, you want to be sure that both boys and girls have *equal access to and encouragement to try* all the activity areas. You don't want little girls subtly pushed into the housekeeping area, while little boys are directed toward the blocks. Are there ties and men's jackets in the dress-up area, as well as skirts and gowns? Are both sexes encouraged to try out "professional" accessories such as firefighter hats or stethoscopes? Do boys and girls both do sewing projects and cooking?

The block area often becomes very territorial among boys, who will try to exclude girls. How do the teachers encourage *all* the youngsters to play with blocks? (See Chapter 5 for why playing with blocks helps a child's intellectual development.)

Staff Specialists

To enrich the curriculum some schools bring in specialists for classes in gymnastics, movement/dance, music/song, Suzuki violin, nature, art. You would not want a program whose curriculum is overwhelmed with these specialty classes, but one or two add to the preschool experience. Check:

NO ONE'S PERFECT

You may well hit an otherwise terrific teacher on a bad day. We've all had them. If you have real questions about how a teacher handled a situation, or if there doesn't seem to be much of a spark in a class, ask the director before you write off the school. Or schedule another visit to the school.

✎ the credentials of the specialists the school uses;
✎ how often classes are held;
✎ how the school handles children who don't want to participate.

The Children

You are not only observing the teachers and staff when you visit a school, you also want to watch the children. They are the best indication if the program is working.

✎ Do the children seem happy? Can you see it in their faces? Are they busy, engaged in their activities?
✎ Can you sense an underlying excitement in the classroom?
✎ If the room is noisy, is it under control? Children may be talking to one another, but is there shouting? Do the children seem to be interacting well with each other? You will probably see plenty of parallel playing, that is children playing *alongside of* each other rather than directly *with* one another, but how well are they handling sharing the same space, toys?
✎ How diverse are the students? Is that important to you? Is there a relatively even number of boys and girls?

The Second Visit

You will want to visit again those schools that impress you. If you prefer to bring your child, discuss the arrangements with the school director. This visit is neither an admissions test nor an orientation opportunity for her. It's a chance for you to see her in the environment. Keep in mind that your child is at least a full year younger than the students, a significant difference in terms of maturity for preschoolers. She may well cry and cling, or she may jump right into the new situation with both feet! Either, both, or something in between is perfectly appropriate behavior.

It's also fine if you prefer not to bring your child to any of the schools before you make a decision. You will have an opportunity to prepare her for the program during the summer by reading books about preschool together, perhaps a visit to the school playground, even meeting with the teacher before classes begin. The opening days of school are also planned to ease the transition (see Chapter 4).

This second visit is an opportunity to refine your observations. Now that you have looked at several schools, you know better what's important to you.

Testing

Except in urban areas, admission to preschool is generally on a first-come, first-served basis. There can be other issues taken into

WHAT IS THE MAKEUP OF THE SCHOOL COMMUNITY?

You want to ask the director about the families whose children attend the school. While you may value socioeconomic, racial-ethnic diversity among the students, you also want to be comfortable in the school community. You probably don't want to be the only family in the school where both parents work outside of the home. Nor would you want to be the only stay-at-home mom. Both might be an isolating experience for you and your child.

Working parents find that nannies/au pairs often develop their own network and make play dates for their charges. Your child may feel more comfortable if she is not the only one who has a nanny or who goes to day care after school. And a school community offers the opportunity for the adults to make friends, as well as the children. For a mother who works outside of the home, this is a chance to build a support network.

YOU NEED TO KNOW

You will want to spend some time with the director before you make a final decision about the school. Ask her:

1. To describe a typical day. This will give you an overview of the program and an insight into what the school considers important.
2. What are the school vacations? Do they observe legal holidays, as well as follow a public-school calendar (this may be important if you have to coordinate the vacation schedules of several children)? Will you find the vacation schedule burdensome if you are relying on the school for child care while you work?
3. What is the enrollment process for the school? Is it first-come, first-served or is there a screening process? Are siblings given preference?
4. What is the age cutoff for each grade? Are there any exceptions?
5. How does the school handle separation? Is there an established formula for slowly introducing the new students to school, and gradually weaning the parent out of the classroom and the school?
6. Does the school regularly schedule parent-teacher conferences?
7. Can you request a specific teacher? Can you request that your child be placed with a specific friend? Can you ask that your child not be placed in the same class as a certain child?

account such as preferences for siblings; membership in the congregation if the school is church/synagogue affiliated; or an effort to keep the boy-girl ratio even.

But some urban independent schools require more before making a decision on whether or not to admit. Some admissions' processes are more high powered than others, and you will need to balance your interest in the school versus your willingness to participate in the process.

Generally, after parents tour the school and apply for admission, more exclusive schools invite the parents for an interview. During the session, which generally lasts less than a half hour, you may be asked about your child's interests; your views on child development/rearing/discipline; your goals for your child; your interest in the school; and your professional lives. The questions tend to be general such as "tell me about your child," and you will want to discuss a special fondness for Legos, or books, or play-Doh. **Don't feel that you have to psychoanalyze your child.** As one mother pointed out: "I love my daughter, but she was only 18 months old. How long could you discuss her interests?" When asked what her goals for preschool were, this mother replied that she hoped her child would become "more independent." You may also be asked for letters of recommendation from other parents whose children attend the school or members of the congregation.

Some schools also screen the child in a group setting. At these meetings, the preschool teachers and/or director observe four to six preschool applicants as they play. They are looking to see how the child interacts in a school environment with other children and with adults.

The horror stories of these preschool observation sessions are legendary. One mother recounts how in the same 45-minute meeting her child hit another youngster, bit a teacher, and refused to share. The little boy was admitted to the school and did fine.

How to Prepare

How can you prepare your child for these observation sessions? **You really can't, and shouldn't.** *What you can do is what you would do whenever you take your child to a new experience.*

1. Talk before you go, in a quiet way, about how you are going someplace new and that it will be fun.
2. Tell your youngster that there will be other children there.
3. Reassure him that Mommy and/or Daddy will be in the next room waiting for him.

TIP: It is important, if at all possible, that both parents attend the interview session. The school wants to know that both parents value and are committed to preschool education.

TIP: Try not to worry or overreact to what happens—these are professionals and they have seen it all. If your child cries, clings, or misbehaves, it doesn't mean that she won't be admitted to the program.

4. Encourage your child to have fun with the toys, kids, teachers, etc.
5. Keep the discussion low key or your child may react to the pressure you are, inadvertently, putting on him.

Even if you believe that admission to this preschool will set your child on a track for admission to prestigious upper schools (which is a whole other question), **the surest way to create a problem is to let your child get a hint of your anxiety.** Again, the preschool staff are professionals. They know how to encourage youngsters to separate from parents (and when to stop if a youngster refuses to cooperate). One mother was worried because her daughter was going through a phase where she pretended that she was Peter Rabbit and would respond only to that name. The teachers were happy to oblige.

Standardized Tests

Some schools may require the young child to take a standardized test as part of the admissions process. Generally this is for admissions to the four-year-old class or part of a pre-K program in an ongoing school. The Stanford-Binet or the Wechsler Preschool and Primary Scales (WPPSI) are the tests normally given to preschool applicants. Although most preschools will use the test as only one criteria for admission, it is difficult not to be concerned about how your child will perform. Schools also take into account reports from the child's current preschool, as well as observation of the child in a group setting and a parents' interview.

It is daunting for many preschoolers to answer a series of questions from a tester, who may be as charming and nonthreatening as Mister Rogers but is, nonetheless, a stranger. Your child may decide he doesn't want to participate. Or your child could test poorly for perfectly logical reasons as one mother discovered. Her daughter, who began reading independently at two and one-half years old, tested poorly because she was a thumb sucker and couldn't manipulate the blocks well with her one remaining (nondominant) hand. Again, you should remember that the tester is a professional who has also seen a wide range of reactions from preschoolers who are hesitant or reluctant to participate. The tester may suggest that the test be taken on another day if your child is having a bad time.

What's on Preschool Standardized Tests?

The tests have several sections including a question and answer portion; manipulative materials for the child to use; and a hands-on "writing" section.

The two most common standardized preschool tests generally take a little more than one hour to administer. As one test professional advised: "The best way to prepare your child is to make sure he has a good night's sleep and eats a good breakfast."

Before coming to the test site, talk to your child, in a low-key way, about where you are going and why. You might say: "We are going to meet a new teacher who wants to talk to you about what four- and five-year-olds can do. I'll be in the next room while you answer some questions, play with some toys, and do a little work with this teacher."

Are These Tests Valid?

Many experts have questions about the validity of these tests. Some schools, such as those associated with a university, use them as part of a research project and don't consider them part of the admissions process. Others use standardized tests if they suspect a problem, such as a hearing or vision deficit, and want it confirmed. It's hard to argue with either of these uses, although the validity of the process is still questionable. Nonetheless, if you choose to apply to a school that requires testing for admission, you must balance the excellence of the program versus your concerns that the school uses these criteria in judging three-year-olds. You may decide that it's worth it. Most of all, remember that these tests are valid only for the time they are given. They can't be used to predict a child's future. As one tester remarked: "The weaknesses at one age might well be the strengths at a later time."

If you disagree with the test results, or believe that there were unusual circumstances during the testing (for example, your child was ill when she took the test), you should notify the school and request a new testing date.

Tuition Fees

An important consideration in choosing a preschool is whether or not you can afford it. Scholarships are limited and federally or locally funded child-care preschool education programs, like Head Start, may have strict income requirements.

Some schools charge by the week, others by the month, and still others require payment either by the term, or even up front

DON'T TAKE IT PERSONALLY

This is the toughest part of a selective admissions process—whether it's preschool or college. Parents can't help but feel that they are being judged. But the decision to admit or not may have nothing to do with how bright your child—or you—are. Schools are trying to create a balanced class or school and the screening process is one way to achieve that. If your daughter is denied admission, it may well be that there were too many girls applying to the school and therefore a girl with a sibling who had previously attended the school was admitted while your child was not.

The most important thing is to remember that you are talking about a preschooler. The final results are not in yet about his intelligence and potential, and it would be a terrible disservice to let the preschool admissions process limit your vision for your child.

for the entire year. The payment plan may make a difference on your budget. One school, which required term payments, worked with a family that couldn't come up with a lump payment. The school treasurer divided the tuition fee by six (the number of months in a term), then asked the parents to make out six checks, sequentially dated for the next six months. Each month the treasurer deposited one of the checks and credited the family's account. This helped the parents' cash flow and reduced the follow-up that the treasurer would have had in order to get monthly payments.

Tuition costs vary enormously across the country. For example, one school in Florida charges $310 a month for three days a week, four hours per day; a Long Island, New York, school charges $90 a month for five days a week two and one-half hours per day. You will have to comparison shop within your own area. Generally speaking, urban areas are more expensive than suburban areas, which are more expensive than rural schools. Two important points:

1. More expensive does not necessarily mean better.
2. But if a school is considerably cheaper than others in the same area, you want to know where they are cutting costs.

Toilet Training Requirements for Admission

Some schools require your child to be toilet trained before she starts the program. Others permit diapers in the toddler classes, but insist that threes or fours have to be trained. And still others have no policy at all.

Sometimes there are local or state health code requirements that order separate changing areas or changing tables for diapering children. A school may decide that it's easier to insist that all students must be trained before school begins. Or a day-care center may not admit an older preschooler who is not toilet trained because the changing table area is in a separate section of the facility and it would be difficult for the staff to accompany a three-

or four-year-old youngster to that area during the day (also possibly embarrassing for the child).

Obviously, this puts pressure on parents and children. You'll need to decide if (1) your child is likely to be trained by the opening of school (2) if not, your alternatives. Will you get a refund if he is not trained in time? Suppose he is partially trained? If your youngster seems to be starting toilet training anyway, then a little extra attention to the effort won't hurt. But don't allow it to become a "battle of wills." It will almost certainly slow down the process.

Like walking, talking, and any other developmental milestone, a child will become toilet trained when she is ready. Some will be ready at two, others at three, and some at four or older. It may be frustrating when every other almost four-year-old you know is out of diapers, but in time, so will yours. For the preschooler who is newly trained, seeing other youngsters use the toilet reinforces the behavior.

In any case, most preschoolers have "accidents" at some time: You'll want to know how the school handles those situations. Certainly there should never be any recriminations or shaming for "accidents." It's also not unusual if your child has more "accidents" when she first starts school, a new routine can throw off even kids who have been trained for months. Similarly, "accidents" often happen when a child is engrossed in play. She doesn't want to take the time out to use the bathroom.

You also want to know how the school reinforces toileting behavior. Generally most schools take the children to the bathroom several times in the morning and a teacher keeps her eyes open for the child who is exhibiting "classic signs" of needing to use the toilet.

Let your child's teacher know where your youngster is in the toilet-training process. If your child has a problem with chronic constipation, the school should probably know since it may affect how your youngster feels about going to the bathroom, especially if she has painful bowel movements. If your child prefers to use a potty seat and the school doesn't have any, then begin to wean her from it before classes begin. Make sure that your child wears clothes that make it easy for her to use the toilet without help. And if your youngster is shy about using the toilet around other children, be sure and tell the teacher so she can arrange for her to use the toilet in private.

Questions and Answers

Q: I chose a preschool after visiting it several times, interviewing the director, and taking my son to visit it as well. I was satisfied with my choice, until my neighbor told me about a disturbing incident that happened at the school several years ago when a child was seriously hurt on the playground. Now I'm really worried. Have I made the wrong choice?

A: Not necessarily. Call up the director and ask her to discuss the incident and what remedies are in place to make sure that it never happens again. While it's understandable that the director did not mention the problem to new parents, she should be willing to be forthright about the incident if asked.

Q: I enrolled my three-year-old daughter for a class that meets three mornings a week. But this summer she attended a local day camp that met five mornings a week and loved it. Do you think she will be bored this fall with a shorter program?

A: The curriculum and goals of preschool and day camp are different. Your daughter won't be bored in a high-quality school program, even if it meets only three mornings a week. She may welcome the "down time," the other mornings, from the intensity of school. That time is also an opportunity for her to explore other interests with you or your caregiver. You might want to enroll her in a gymnastics or movement program, visit the library for story hour, arrange a play date, or best of all, allow her time to play and putter around the house. We need to give young children time to just be by themselves. We don't need to offer 24-hour entertainment.

Q: We're interested in enrolling our son in a private preschool that requires a parents' interview, as well as a separate observation of our child. We both work and can arrange time off for the interview, but can our nanny take our son to the observation class?

A: Generally, the answer is yes. As long as your son is comfortable going to new places with his caregiver, it should be fine. One mother remembers that the first year she applied for her daughter's admission to a preschool, she arranged time off from work to accompany the child on the observation visit, dressed both the child and herself carefully, and thought the class had gone well. Furthermore, she and her husband both took off time to attend the parents' interview. The little girl was not accepted into the program. The following year, again applying for admission to the same preschool, the mother sent the little girl with her baby-sitter to the observation class and when her husband was unable to attend, went to the parents' interview alone. This time the child was accepted. The point is that there are many criteria a competitive, private preschool considers when deciding admissions—and you don't necessarily know what the school's needs are in any one year.

Q: **I really like this preschool in my town, but it's much more expensive than other schools in the area. I can't afford the fees, but do preschools offer scholarships?**

A: You'll never know unless you ask. Some schools actually do have scholarships in order to attract a diverse student body. It's not unusual for schools to have a sliding fee scale for families in need. Another option is to offer some service to the school in exchange for a reduced fee. Some of the services you might provide include: driving other children to school (check your car insurance); classroom aide (in a class other than your child's); bookkeeping responsibilities; landscaping or snow removal.

3

THE DAY-CARE DILEMMA

You don't have to sacrifice a quality preschool program in order to get excellent day care. If traditional preschool hours (three hours in the morning or afternoon) do not meet your child-care needs, look for a full workday program that provides both an organized preschool program *and* quality day care. It adds a component to your search. You will want to observe not only how the school handles all the issues discussed in earlier chapters, but also how they deal with meals, naps, toileting, and the long hours that children and teachers will be together.

Or you may decide that you don't want to put your child in a full-day program. In that case, your requirements for a preschool may still need to include: whether it is in a convenient location for your sitter; whether there are other families in the school where both parents work outside the home; how effectively the teachers work with child-care providers to make your child feel comfortable.

Nearly 60 percent of women who have children under the age of three work outside the home, and the day-care dilemma is being confronted every day by families across the country. You will be able to find both a quality program and good child care, but it may take more effort. And without question, it will cost more to get the coverage you need.

HOW WILL DAY CARE AFFECT THE PARENT-CHILD RELATIONSHIP?

Many parents worry that placing their child in day care for many hours a week will weaken the parent-child attachment. A new study of more than 1,000 infants and their mothers offers reassurance. Researchers found that the sense of trust felt by 15-month old children for their mothers was not affected by whether or not they were in day care, or by how many hours they spent there. The study also found that the mother-child bond was unaffected by the age the youngster entered day care, the quality or type of care, or even how many times care arrangements were changed. Rather, a mother's sensitivity and responsiveness to her child is the foundation for strong attachment and trust. It is the *quality* of the parent-child relationship that is crucial.

Child-Care Options

Even if you already have good child-care arrangements in place, as you begin your search for a preschool program, it's a good time to reconsider your options. Your child's needs are changing, and you will want to be sure that your child-care choice is appropriate for a preschooler. The primary focus, whichever child-care option you choose, continues to be the individuals you have elected to be caregivers.

Your basic child-care options are:

- ✎ **A day-care center,** an institution that operates a full-workday schedule.
- ✎ **A family day-care home,** typically a woman who watches a few children in her home. The sitter may be responsible for watching your child before and after school, as well as getting your youngster to and from preschool.
- ✎ **In-home child care,** a sitter (nanny, au pair) to come into your home (whether as a live-in or as a daily worker). She may not only watch your child, but also may also be responsible for household chores.

✎ In your search for a child-care provider your decision comes down to how you answer one basic question: Is the person or day-care center you have chosen to watch your child *loving, responsive, and skillful at interacting with a preschooler?*

Your job may be simple if you find only one situation where you can truthfully answer yes. Then your best bet is to work out the arrangements around this individual or center. But you may well have several acceptable choices, in which case, there are advantages and disadvantages to each type of child care. You have to determine the right combination for your family.

A WORD ABOUT REFERENCES

No matter what child-care option you choose, checking references is vitally important.

1. It will be terrific if you can call families you know, but otherwise ask for a list of families that currently use the caregiver (or day-care center).
2. Check with families who no longer have children in the program. You'll want to know why, although the explanation may be as simple as changing child-care needs.
3. Do not rely on written references—confirm any letter with a follow-up phone call.
4. If the caregiver or center is licensed, ask to see the current license or registration; if it isn't licensed, check with local authorities to see if a license is necessary.
5. If you use an agency to find a caregiver: check out the reputation of the business (ask the agency for references); how long have they been in business; what they do if a match does not work out. Call the Better Business Bureau to see if the agency has had any complaints lodged against it.
6. If you find a caregiver through an agency, even if the company has screened the candidates, you still need to do your own reference check.

Your Child's Role in Choosing Child Care

The selection of an appropriate child-care giver, whether it's a center, a family day-care home, or an in-home sitter, is fundamentally a parental decision. But include your child in part of the decision-making process. Introduce your child to any prospective candidate. Take her to visit any day-care center or family day-care home that you consider a likely prospect. It's probably better for you to visit the centers or homes at least once **without** your child. This gives you the chance to thoroughly investigate the facility.

When your child meets the prospective sitter, look for the following:

1. If your child is shy with strangers, how does the sitter handle the situation?
2. Does the sitter seem comfortable and respectful of your youngster's reluctance to interact?
3. Does she know how to engage a preschooler? Does she get down on her level to talk?
4. Compatibility: you're not looking for a clone of your child, but someone who complements her personality. If you have a very active youngster, you'll want a sitter or day-care provider who can keep up with your child's energy level. At the same time, you want a sitter who also will encourage your child in other directions as well, making time for stories, art projects, and other quiet activities.

The Day-Care Center

Daycare centers may have as few as 30 children or as many as several hundred. The national average is 84. They may be run as a nonprofit program by groups such as churches, community organizations, universities, or local government; or may be operated as for-profit businesses by individuals or corporations. Who "owns" the day-care center is of less importance than how it is administered.

The Advantages

✎ **Coverage**   When you need child care from 7:30 in the morning until 6:00 in the evening, not only during the academic year, but during school vacations and the summer, a day-care center may be the best place to get that kind of coverage. If your place of business expects you at work, even if schools are closed because of the weather, there is a sense of security knowing that the center will be open. As any working parent knows, that is a major advantage.

✎ **Variety**   Your child will probably meet a greater assortment of children in a well-run day-care center than either in family day care or with an individual sitter. This gives your child an opportunity to interact with a variety of youngsters, making it more likely that she will meet a few who share common interests. It also increases the likelihood that parents will find a community of other families with young children.

✎ **Standards**   According to a survey by the American Academy of Pediatrics, day-care centers "have better regulations for health, safety, sanitation, and nutrition than family day-care homes." It's important to remember, however, that licensing requirements generally reflect the *minimum* standards you want. Any center you choose should exceed those health, safety, and sanitation requirements. Day-care center workers, especially directors and teachers, have more training in child development and more opportunities for training.

✎ **Convenience**   A good day-care center is, in some ways, one-stop shopping. You don't have to worry about getting your child from home to school to child care. She's in one place, you write one check, and you only have to deal with one set of teachers and caregivers.

Disadvantages

✎ **High turnover**   One estimate is that more than 40 percent of day-care staff will change jobs each year. That's hard on kids who need the continuity of care. Look for a strong director to help ease the transition periods for the children. Ask the director what is the center's staff turnover rate and how the center handles the problem. If you find a center where the turnover rate is low—that's a good sign.

- ✎ **Group size** While the National Association for the Education of Young Children sets guidelines for preschool group sizes (see Chapter 2), some day-care centers tend to organize around the outside limits.
- ✎ **Institutional character** This is both a plus and a minus when considering a center. A good day-care center shouldn't feel institutional, but there is no question it's not a family home. Day-care centers may be somewhat busier than a family home with fewer children, but the staff should be as loving and caring as you would find in the best family day-care center or with an individual sitter. Day-care center staff, some research has shown, may be better able to cope with the demands of many children because they have ready backup in case of emergency or psychological burnout. Women who run family day care often get irritable or more restrictive in their care of young children because they are alone with children all day and don't have a second adult to relieve them or share the experience.

Family Day Care

It's hard to know exactly how many children are in family day-care situations. One study estimates that over 3.6 million children are in regulated family day care, but that is just the tip of the iceberg. The numbers don't reflect youngsters, probably two out of three, who are cared for by unlicensed day-care providers.

Advantages

- ✎ **Homelike atmosphere** Family day care, when it is good, mimics a home—your home. The caregiver watches a limited number of children in her home, with a very personalized approach to the needs of each child and her family. You may be able to establish a closer relationship with the caregiver.
- ✎ **Less expensive** Generally, family day care is less expensive than either day-care centers or a sitter who comes to your home.

✎ **Flexibility** Depending upon the preferences of your caregiver, a family day-care provider may be more flexible about sick children and late pick up than a day-care center. Many centers charge significant fees for late pick ups and may be adamant about not staying past a specific hour. A family day-care provider may be able to accommodate demanding business schedules. Also, for those times when your child can't go to school, but is not seriously ill (a bad cold, the additional day after the fever has broken), your family day-care provider may be willing to allow the child to stay in her home while you go to work.

Disadvantages

✎ **Burnout** Child care is a demanding, underappreciated, underpaid job. The turnover rate is high, but unlike a day-care center, if your family day-care provider decides to quit offering her services, you have to make new arrangements for your child, putting her into a new setting, with new friends.

✎ **Coverage** Will you have coverage if your child-care provider gets sick, wants to take a vacation, has an emergency? Is she responsible for arranging backup coverage or are you?

✎ **Standards** Family day-care workers generally do not have formal training in early childhood development. Since most family day-care homes are unlicensed, the health and safety standards are up to the individual caregiver.

✎ **Adult-child ratio** Licensed family day-care homes are permitted, by many states, a higher ratio of children to adult than is permitted in day-care centers. If unlicensed, the number of children watched by a single adult is determined by the family day-care worker and often exceeds the recommended number.

Transition to Home

After a long day in preschool and/or day care, coming home is not always easy—for parent or child. You're tired and still face an evening of child- and home-care. Your child is also weary and may have trouble making the transition from one location to another. It's not anyone's best moment.

It's not a reflection on you if your child frequently throws a temper tantrum, begins to whine, seems to revert to babyish behavior, or ignores you when you pick him up from day care. Any and all of these reactions are typical.

Here are some tips (parent tested) to help with the transition:

1. Don't be in a rush when you pick him up. Although you may feel pressured to get him home, start dinner, and have some "quality" time together, your child will react better if the transition is smooth and calm. Allow him, if possible, to finish whatever project or game he is doing.
2. Don't be late at pick up. It only adds to his anxiety.
3. Permit him to show you what he has been doing during the day. Perhaps even linger over a book he particularly likes or an art project he completed. You want to integrate both his worlds.
4. Keep a healthy snack in the car for the ride home. It helps fight the hunger that, if combined with fatigue, may add up to trouble.

In-Home Child Care

You may opt to hire someone to baby-sit your child in your own home. You may choose an experienced nanny, a teenage au pair who lives with the family and baby-sits in exchange for a small stipend, or a day worker. You may want the sitter strictly to focus on child-care responsibilities or you may expect the sitter to do light housekeeping as well.

Advantages

✎ **Flexibility** If negotiated at the outset, you can adapt the sitter's schedule to your needs. If you are going to work late, your child is already in her own home. If you choose to have the sitter come early in the morning (or if she lives in), some of the morning "crazies" can be reduced as there is an extra pair of hands.

✎ **Convenience** Your child does not have to leave the comfort and security of her own home. If your child is sick, she can stay at home with the sitter while you go to work.

✎ **Household chores** Most families ask the sitter to help with light housekeeping, such as the children's laundry or straightening up the playroom. Other sitters assume much more responsibility for household chores. Again this can be negotiated at the outset. In any case, having someone to help, however limited, is one less burden for the parents.

✎ **Less exposure to infections** This is less of an advantage since your child will be in preschool at least part of the time. But in general, children who are cared for in their own home have a more limited exposure to sick youngsters.

Disadvantages

✎ **Social interaction** Depending on how energetic or how inclined your sitter is, your child's outside contacts may be limited. Of course, with your youngster in preschool, she will at least be playing with other children during class. But it will be up to your sitter to make sure that she has play dates—and that the play dates go well.

✎ **Supervision** Parents worry about their child's safety, whether they are watched by a sitter, in family day care, or enrolled in a day-care center. The concern here is that with a sitter at home, there are no other child-care workers to act as checks and balances.

✎ **Standards** Sitters generally do not have formal training in early childhood development.

✎ **Cost** Hiring a sitter to come into your home is more expensive. A live-in nanny is probably the most expensive, but even an au pair, a mother's helper who receives a smaller stipend in exchange for room and board, is still costly. Remember, you are feeding another adult.

✎ **Privacy** If you choose to hire someone to live in, you will trade convenience for privacy.

A WORD ABOUT TAXES

If you and your spouse are both working at least part-time (or are full-time students), you may be eligible for a tax credit for child-care expenses. Single parents who work are also eligible. Check with the Internal Revenue Service for the most current regulations and computation schedule.

According to Julian Block, author of *Julian Block's Tax Avoidance Secrets* (Boardroom, 1996), you can count in-home sitters or outside-the-home (preschool, family day care or day-care center) expenses that permit you to work or actively search for a job. The credit is a dollar-for-dollar subtraction from the tax you would otherwise owe.

Claiming the credit is easy if your child is in a preschool (tuition can be counted as a child-care expense) or in a family day care or day-care center that reports the income. The problem will be if you choose to use a family day-care sitter that chooses (illegally) to work "off the books." In that case, if you claim the deduction, you put the sitter at risk should the IRS reconcile your tax claim with hers. Similarly, if you elect to pay your in-home sitter "off the books" (also illegal), and claim the child-care tax credit, then you risk being audited and penalized.

When you are choosing which child-care option best meets your needs, keep in mind the tax advantages—or disadvantages—of each.

The Search for Child Care

The basic requirements for good child-care are the same whichever option you choose. You want a good fit for your child **and** you. You need to be comfortable with the child-care choice you make in order to work effectively at the office. You are searching for a center or individual who will be *loving, responsive, and skillful at interacting with your child*, who can work the hours you need, and who you can afford.

Where to Start

First, you need to figure out your child-care budget. With your child ready to start preschool, you need to determine how much tuition is going to cost and add that to the cost of child care. That figure may determine if you are going to look for a day-care center that combines preschool with after-class child care; or whether you can afford to send your child to a private preschool and pay separately for child care at a center, in a family day-care home, or with a sitter you hire. Once you have your budget, you can then begin to survey your options.

Next, as with choosing a preschool, develop a list of centers, family day-care homes, or sitters from a variety of sources and begin the search.

To Choose a Day-Care Center

Accredited, Licensed Centers

The National Association for the Education of Young Children (NAEYC) will provide a list of accredited centers in your area. Send a self-addressed, stamped envelope to NAEYC, 1834 Connecticut Avenue, N.W., Washington, DC 20009. However, accreditation is voluntary and the number of centers involved is small. You may find an excellent day-care center that is not NAEYC accredited. It's worth checking out each center and judging each on its merits.

Day-care centers must be licensed and your state's day-care licensing board (check under the Department of Health and Human Services or the Welfare Department) can provide a list of child-care referral agencies.

Check the yellow pages under nurseries, day care, preschools, and nursery schools for additional names for your list. Then check with the local authorities to be sure they are licensed. Friends, diaper services, pediatricians, local churches/synagogues, bulletin boards in supermarkets and baby clothes/furniture stores, and the local newspaper are all possible resources to compile a full list of possible day-care centers. Word of mouth is good, but, of course, trust your own eyes to determine if a place that is "great" for one family meets *your family's needs*.

Start with a Phone Call

You can narrow your list significantly if you ask some of the basic questions over the phone. You'll want to ask:

- ✎ Location
- ✎ Hours
- ✎ Number of children enrolled in center
- ✎ Adult/child ratio
- ✎ Grouping (by age? developmental level? hours?) for both preschool program and day-care program
- ✎ Fees
- ✎ Vacation Schedule

If the answers to these basic questions meet your needs, then you are ready to schedule a visit.

The Visit

A day-care center needs to have the same interesting, warm, inviting, **safe** environment that a quality preschool has—and more. It has to be a home away from home. You need to check out how the center handles the rhythm of the day: meals, rest time, long, winter afternoons shut indoors, etc. Your child may be spending 8 to 10 hours a day at the center—how will she and the staff use the time well.

You will want to schedule at least two visits to the center. The checklist provided (see Chapter 2) will give you guidelines for evaluating the preschool program the center provides. But then schedule another visit for more difficult periods of the day. For example, how does the center manage lunchtime; the period before nap time; late afternoon when children are getting tired and cranky. If they can handle these transitions well, you can feel more comfortable about how they handle the more routine parts of the day.

Other points to add to the checklist:

SAFETY

Sanitary conditions in the diaper changing area and kitchen are a serious issue in day-care centers. Children under the age of three in day-care contract about 30 percent more gastrointestinal ailments (such as diarrhea) than children who stay at home. You want to know:

✎ Is the diaper-changing area separated from the food area?

✎ Is it sanitized after each use?

✎ Are dirty diapers stored in sealed, plastic-lined bins?

✎ Do employees wash their hands before and after changing diapers?

✎ Do employees and children wash their hands before eating?

DAY-CARE PROGRAM

You don't want to have all the interesting activities packed into the morning and the afternoon disorganized. On the other hand, you don't want your child so scheduled that there isn't any "down" time.

✎ Is the full-day program as complete as the morning program?

✎ What is the center's balance between structure and freedom?

✎ How do they handle the transition when part-time children are picked up at the end of the morning program? Children staying the full day may become anxious when other parents begin picking up their children. Are the full-day children already out of the room and into another activity (lunch)?

FOOD

Meals are an important part of a child's day.

✎ Ask to see a weekly menu. Don't be unhappy if there is not much variety. In fact, it's reassuring if the center is relying on kid-favorite items like grilled cheese, peanut butter, hamburgers, pizza. At least they will be eaten. What you are looking for are healthy, balanced meals and snacks.

A TYPICAL DAY IN A DAY-CARE CENTER

7:00–9:00 A.M.	Children arrive, at different times, during this period. They may have breakfast (cold cereals, milk, fruit, toast). Puzzles, books, toys are available.
9:00–12:00	Preschool day (see page 114)
12:00–12:45	Lunch
12:45–1:00	Cleanup, toileting, brush teeth, get ready for rest time.
1:00–2:30	Nap or rest time on individual cots
2:30–3:00	Children awake, quiet activities
3:00–3:15	Snack
3:30–4:15	Outdoor play
4:15–5:30	Indoor play with toys, books, puzzles, paints
5:30–6:00	Story time, dismissal

✎ Ask if your child can bring food from home. If the center provide meals, they may discourage it.

✎ Are meals family style with the adults sitting, eating, and chatting with the children?

✎ Does the slow eater feel rushed?

NAPPING

Some youngsters still need to snooze in the afternoon, and even those children who no longer take a regular nap benefit from quiet time after lunch. How does the center handle rest time?

✎ What kind of cots or mats do the children use?

✎ Can they have their favorite blanket or stuffed animal with them?

✎ Are children assigned their own specific mat (to cut down on head-lice transmission)?

✎ Is the room dark and quiet enough to accommodate nappers?

✎ Can those children who don't sleep play quietly on their cots or look at books?

COMMUNICATION

Since your child is going to spend a large chunk of his day at the center, you want to be sure and keep open the lines of communication with the staff. You'll want to hear what he has done all day, what he's eaten, whether or not he slept. This is not only to keep tabs on your child, but this kind of information gives the parents conversational openers for their children. Furthermore, the staff who care for your child in the morning may not be the same individuals you see at the evening pick up. A written note helps bridge the gap.

Conversely, the center staff needs to have information from you about your child. Whether it's through a written note or a few words before you leave, share important information with the center staff. Tell the staff if your child has had a difficult night and may be exhausted as the day goes on. It makes their job easier—and most importantly helps your child.

Many day-care centers have written forms that the staff and parents complete on a daily basis. They may be detailed or brief, including not only quantifiable information like how much your child ate, but also incidents that may affect his mood that evening or exciting events that you should know about. It doesn't take away

RECOMMENDATIONS

Ask the day-care center director for the names of parents whose children are *currently* enrolled. When you speak to the families ask direct questions:

- What do you like best about the center?
- What do you like least?
- Have you had any problems—and how were they resolved?
- Have you had any special requests—and was the staff receptive?
- Has this family heard about any of the other centers you are considering? Did they consider any of them? Why did they choose this particular center?

from one-on-one dialogue, but can give you the information you want at a glance.

- ✎ Does the center have a written form? How complete is it?
- ✎ Does the staff encourage informal conversations (not to replace formal parent-teacher conferences)?
- ✎ Can you call during the day to check on your child? Can you speak to her?

Family Day Care

Family day care generally refers to a group of children who are cared for by a single individual in the caregiver's home. Some family day-care homes are licensed, but the vast majority run an informal arrangement, often with payment "off the books." While no one knows exactly how many children are in family day-care homes, it is considered to be the most widely used form of child care.

Logistics

If you choose to send your child to preschool and then use a family day-care home to watch her for the rest of the workday, then your logistics may be more complicated. Before you commit to either a preschool or a family day-care provider, you need to figure out how to make it all work.

- ✎ **Transportation** Who is responsible? If your sitter is going to either take or pick up at preschool, what happens if she gets sick; or if one of her other charges is ill; or her car breaks down? *What is your backup plan?*

  Give your sitter a list of local friends she can call in an emergency. Include on the list the number of a local taxi service in case your sitter has automotive troubles.

  If your sitter is going to be responsible for transportation (not just for preschool, but for any trips), make sure she has a car seat for your child—and that she insists that your child is always safely buckled in. Check your insurance—and hers—to make sure she is covered for transporting children.

✎ **Play dates** Will your sitter welcome play dates your child wants to have? Although most don't, especially if they are watching other children, you'll want to know under what circumstances a classmate can come to play; do you have to pay additional fees if your child has a play date at your sitter's home? Also negotiate whether you pay when your child goes to another child's home for a play date. Will your sitter pick up your child from a play date or will the other child's mother have to provide the transportation?

To Find a Family Day-Care Home

Most parents find a family day-care home by word of mouth. Some see a listing on a bulletin board in a church/synagogue, supermarket, library, etc.

But the National Association for Family Child Care accredits family day-care homes and will send you a list of day-care referral agencies and day-care provider support groups in your state and local area. Send a stamped, self-addressed envelope to NAFCC Accreditation, P.O. Box 161489, Fort Worth, TX 76161. Again, like day-care centers, accreditation is a voluntary process and most family day-care providers, even excellent ones, have not sought accreditation.

Routine

Just because this is a home, rather than an institution, doesn't mean that there shouldn't be some routine to the day. While flexibility is important, you want the child-care provider to offer more than just a room full of toys. She should be interacting with your youngster, perhaps cooking or doing crafts together, taking your child to the park. Even though your youngster will get a full morning of stimulation at preschool, the long afternoon hours should not be spent parked in front of the television. Even if the shows or videos are "educational," that's not enough. **You'll want to ask about television viewing when you interview the family day-care provider.**

Other Questions to Ask

✎ Check the caregiver's credentials. Since you are looking for more than someone who can dial 911, you want to know how much *experience* she has had dealing with young children. Does she have an educational background in early childhood education? Ask how long she has been providing family day care and why she chose this profession.

✎ Are the sitter's children part of the child-care group? If they are, you'll want to meet them. Talk about how well her own children have adjusted to the group situation.

✎ What is the sitter's backup plan if either she or her children get sick? Are you responsible for making a backup plan in that eventuality? If it's your responsibility, does the sitter have any suggestions? How often did she take unexpected time off in the previous year?

✎ What is the age range of children in the group? It's not impossible for a caregiver to watch both infants and preschoolers, but you need someone who can balance diverse demands. Childproofing a home for a crawling infant may limit the space and toys available to a preschooler. Will waiting for an infant to wake up from a nap interfere with your child's schedule or routine? Ask the caregiver how she handles these issues.

✎ Does the caregiver's homeowner insurance cover possible injury to a child in her care?

In-Home Child Care

You may prefer to hire a baby-sitter to come into your home on a daily basis or have someone live in with your family. An experienced live-in nanny is probably the most expensive child-care option. An au pair, either from a foreign country or from the United States, usually costs less, but, if she is hired through a licensed agency, may have limits on the numbers of hours she is available to sit. A day worker, depending on the arrangements you make, may be flexible enough to meet your needs, but can present problems if she gets sick or has transportation problems on the day you need to be in the office. Again, backup plans should be made **before** you need them.

Where to Find a Sitter

You find an in-home sitter in much the same way as you do for a family day-care provider or a day-care center. You start with the people you know and then broaden your search. There are employment agencies and au pair agencies, as well. Using one may increase your costs, since the fees can be substantial, but may help develop your list of choices. Good agencies (check their references and reputation first), will screen candidates, run background checks, etc. But you will have to check references as well. Ask any agency about their fees, screening processes, placement success, matching methods, and refund policies.

Basic Work Agreement

Before you interview any sitter, develop a list of the duties you expect performed, the days and hours you expect the sitter to work, the salary and benefits you are prepared to offer. Give the list to all candidates you interview so that you both have a clear idea of how the job will work **before** there is an offer of employment.

Since negotiations are a two-way street, you'll want to listen to the demands of a good candidate. She may want a higher salary or shorter hours—and you may be willing to alter your list to accommodate her needs. And, of course, over a period of time, your needs and the sitter's requirements may change. But the best working relationships begin with clear expectations.

Specifically you'll need to decide:

Salary: What is the base salary (hourly or weekly)? Will you pay overtime? Will you pay a bonus for overtime? Will you offer compensatory time off for overtime? Include a discussion of payment of withholding and unemployment taxes, as well as Social Security payments.

Benefits: How much vacation will you offer? Does it need to be taken when your family takes a vacation? Are you prepared to pay health insurance benefits? Disability insurance?

WHEN SITTERS LIVE IN

If a sitter is going to live with your family, be clear about the accommodations **before** she accepts the job. Privacy is an important issue—for both your family and the sitter. Ideally the sitter's bedroom, with private bath if possible, will be on a separate floor from the family's sleeping quarters.

You also want to establish the ground rules for the use of the telephone, family car, television, etc. You need to discuss whether the sitter can invite guests to your home and whether she may have overnight guests at any time.

In addition you need to decide:

- Will the sitter eat her meals with the family?
- Will she clean up after meals?
- Will she have the same days off each week or will they vary?
- Will she stay in your home during her days off or be expected to leave when she is not on duty?
- Will she celebrate holidays with you (if she is an au pair from abroad that could be part of the cultural exchange)?

Duties: Do you expect the sitter to do light housekeeping chores including laundry, shopping, preparing meals? Will you hire additional household help for heavy cleaning? What do you expect her to do during the hours your child is in school?

Driving: Will the sitter be responsible for driving your child to school, play dates, lessons? Will she use your car or her own? Will you pay for gas and tolls? Can she use your car for her own errands?

If You Decide to Use an Au Pair from a Foreign Country

There are eight approved au pair agencies recognized by the United States government. Established as a cultural exchange program, it's an opportunity for young men and women from abroad to live in the United States, practice their English, earn money, and experience

American family life. In exchange, American families are enriched by child-care givers from foreign countries.

The advantages for American families include: a ready source of screened caregivers; the opportunity to enrich their family life with a caregiver from another culture; less expensive child care.

The disadvantages include: the problems with having any non-family member live in your home on a full-time basis; potential culture clashes; having a fairly young caregiver, which can mean dealing with adolescent behavior; limited work time (au pairs are not permitted to work more than 45 hours per week); having to hire a new sitter every year because an au pair's visa is only good for one year.

If you decide to hire a foreign au pair, here's what you need to know.

1. **Visa**   A foreign au pair will need a visa, which is good for only one year, plus one month of travel. The au pair agency should only provide candidates who have the necessary legal documents.

2. **Changing sitters**   You will have to decide how great an impact it will be on your family to replace the sitter each year. An older preschooler may have a better understanding and ability to adjust to a new sitter than a younger one who becomes very attached to her caregiver.

3. **English fluency**   While one of the incentives of the job for many au pairs is to become more fluent in English, you want an individual who can communicate effectively with your child and with you. It's a wonderful benefit if your child learns a second language from your au pair, but the sitter must be able to speak English well enough to cope with an emergency, call a doctor (or 911), or speak to other children who are visiting for a play date.

4. **Interview**   Conduct a telephone interview before a candidate leaves for the United States. One family, who has hired French au pairs for several years, has the current au pair interview the potential replacement in her native language. Then the parents conduct a separate interview and compare notes with their current sitter.

5. **If it's not working**   While you want to give the au pair and your family a chance to adjust, make a decision sooner rather than later

if it appears that the situation isn't going to work out. In two weeks, as one mother explains, she knew a Danish au pair just wasn't going to meet her family's needs. "I was left having to start the search process all over again—an emotional and financial pain. But although it wouldn't have been a total disaster if she had stayed, I knew I would have spent the entire year dissatisfied."

6. **Driving**   If your sitter is going to be responsible for driving your child places, check your insurance coverage. Does she need a separate policy? Even more important, is she a good driver? If she is British, is she comfortable and competent with driving on the left side of the road? One family paid for a driving lesson for their au pair—that way they got a professional evaluation of her competency.

Questions and Answers

Q: My neighbor and I both work full time. We are considering sharing an in-home sitter, but our children go to separate preschools. Are we just asking for problems?

A: This might be the perfect solution to the child-care needs of both families, assuming you find the right sitter who's willing to take the job **and you and the sitter take the time to work out the logistics.** This is more complicated than if you were asking a sitter to watch more than one child in the same family. Now you are asking a child-care giver to balance the needs, expectations, and schedules of two different groups. It can work, but besides issues of compensation and benefits, here's what you have to resolve:

1.   Is the sitter responsible for driving and picking up at preschool both children and is this feasible? Are there alternatives to the driving dilemma, for example, can alternative car-pool arrangements be made? Is preschool transportation available?

2.   Where will the sitter watch the children? Will you alternate homes?

3.   What are your backup plans if one of the children is ill? Can the sitter watch both children if one is recovering from a mild illness?

4. How compatible are the two children? Even if they are good friends, how will they get along if they have to spend a large amount of time together on a daily basis? Will the children be encouraged to have separate play dates with classmates?

Q: The day-care center we've chosen for our son is excellent, but they are really strict about late pickups, charging an enormous penalty and frankly making clear their disapproval. Sometimes being late is out of my control, traffic jams, etc. Is there any way to make the center more flexible?

A: It's unlikely that you can get the center to adjust its hours unless a majority of the parents make the demand. So one possibility is to see if there are other parents in a similar situation and discuss with the center director extending the hours—perhaps still paying a premium for the extra time, but building it into the center's schedule.

But assuming that is not possible, then you have to figure out your options. First, if you are generally happy with the day-care center, then you need to develop a backup plan for those days you are going to be even just a few minutes late. Can your partner pick up your child? Can another family take your youngster to their home and you pick him up there (even if you offer to pay for the service)? Is one of the center's employees willing to baby-sit?

Practically speaking, you might want to invest in a cellular telephone if traffic jams are an unfortunate part of your life. Although the service can be expensive, you can at least be in contact with the day-care center and alert them to your problem, as well as set in motion your backup plan.

Q: My almost three-year-old daughter readily naps at her day-care center, but refuses to sleep at home during the weekends. Why does she sleep during school days and not on the weekends?

A: This is a common scenario for preschoolers. A well-planned early childhood program, even though it may appear unpressured, is tiring for a youngster. Following a class schedule, moving from one activity to another, separating from parents, and cooperating with classmates can be exhausting for a preschooler. Also teachers and day-care centers know how to set the stage for naps. The room is darkened, security objects (toys, blankets) are distributed, and most important of all, *no one insists that a child sleep, just that she rest.* Some children will spend the rest time playing quietly on their mat; others need the sleep and wake refreshed. When your child is at home during the weekends, the schedule is more flexible, she is able to relax and move at her own pace. If you feel that either your daughter or you need some quiet time in the afternoon, set up a time period when she rests or plays quietly in her room. Your daughter may fall asleep or simply use the time to recharge her energy (as you recharge yours!).

Q: **My four-year-old son's day-care center has worked out perfectly. But I'm expecting a new baby and will be home for at least three months on maternity leave. Should I keep my son home with me? I plan to enroll the new baby in the center when I return to work.**

A: It depends on your finances, but if you can afford to continue sending your son to day-care, even on a part-time basis, it would probably be best for everyone. First, it would provide continuity for your son. In the midst of major changes in the household, the center remains a constant. Furthermore, your son will benefit from continuing in a good preschool program. You can't replicate the activities and social relationships available. Even if he is there on only a part-time basis, it will eliminate the reentry problems you would confront if you withdrew him from the program and then reentered him at a later point. Finally, frankly you can use the one-on-one time with your new baby.

You may hear some complaints or concerns from your son about the time you are spending with the new baby. He may initially resist going to school while you are home on maternity leave. This is normal sibling rivalry and is best treated with reassurance and comfort. Keeping him at home, however, is not the answer. In fact, it may reinforce the idea that something will happen if he is away from you.

4

READY, SET, GO:
THE OPENING DAYS
OF SCHOOL

It may feel like, and in fact may well be, a year or more since you selected a preschool for your child. No doubt your youngster has changed a lot in the intervening months. You can literally and figuratively see the growth.

She may be two inches taller, five pounds heavier. Her language is more complex, and she is able to express herself more clearly with a larger vocabulary. You probably find that as her large-motor skills have developed that translates into long tiring days for you, her parents. Where once she could barely walk, now she runs and climbs endlessly. Her small-motor skills are also more refined. You see it at mealtime when she can feed herself and can effectively use a spoon. You notice it when she turns the pages of the book, grasping the pages easily with just the thumb and forefinger. If she cannot yet fully dress herself, she probably has discovered how to undress herself. And there is so much more. Soon it will be the opening days of preschool and your baby, believe it or not, is ready for the next big step! Here's how to help her be ready for this new experience.

Acknowledge Your Own Feelings

Sending your child off to school for the first time may provoke a range of parental emotions. You may be proud, excited, and happy. If you have been at home with your child, you may also feel relief at the thought of a few hours of freedom several mornings a week. And you may feel guilt that you feel that way. You may worry that your child isn't ready for school, emotionally or developmentally. You may feel depressed that your child is no longer a baby. Yes, he is still little, but he is old enough to go to school and that marks a new stage in his life and yours. You may feel all, some, or none of these emotions—and you may feel them at the same time or successively. It's all very *normal* to have any of these feelings. And it is just as normal if you don't.

What Your Child May Be Feeling

In the weeks before school starts, your child may also be experiencing a myriad of emotions. She may be excited, confused, worried, even bewildered. She may not verbalize any of these feelings. Her language skills may not permit it. You need to recognize that it would be perfectly reasonable for any child to be excited about a strange place everyone keeps insisting will be a lot of fun, but at the same time, does not provide the stability and comfort of what she already knows. It's normal for a child to feel that school is both exciting and a little scary—like any brand-new experience.

Before School Begins

Preparing your child for preschool is a delicate balance. On the one hand you want to talk about what's new in her life, to ease the transition. You want your youngster to be comfortable with beginning a new experience.

On the other hand, you don't want to overdo the preparation. With too much discussion of the subject, school may begin to take on mythic proportions. Your child's fantasies and expectations may never match reality, leading to disappointment. Even worse, your child may become frightened that school needs this big buildup from grown-ups!

Add to the mix that children have wonderful radar. They will pick up *your* concerns and fears, even if you never say a discouraging word. So be careful how often and which words you choose when talking about school.

Work the topic into your conversations naturally. For example, you might point out the school and playground when you pass them in the course of running errands. Talk about the climbing equipment and how to get to the top, or the fastest route to the base. Try it out if possible.

Similarly, while you will want to read books about starting school to your youngster, you don't want to focus exclusively on these subject books. If you read three books together before your child goes to sleep, then each night select only one that talks about school.

Pick up on your child's subtle (and sometimes not so subtle) cues. If the books on school seem to be a turnoff, drop the subject for a few days. It may be overwhelming your youngster.

Most important, **never use school as a threat**. One father, in his zeal to get his daughter toilet trained, informed his two-year-old that she couldn't go to school if she still wore diapers. It was confusing two complex issues. Children have mixed feelings about giving up diapers. The little girl may already have had concerns about school and now learns that it is a place that insists that you change so dramatically (in the child's eyes) before you can attend.

Some Dos

Do try to meet your child's teacher before school begins.

Do talk about the teacher and school in a positive way. This lets your child know that you think school is a safe, exciting place for him to be.

Do try and arrange a play date with a classmate even before school starts. It helps make the transition to a new program a little easier if there is a familiar face in the room.

Do play games like peekaboo and hide-and-seek with your toddler to accustom her to the idea that a parent can go away and then comes back.

Do arrive on time at school (or even slightly early) to allow your child time to adjust before the throng of children arrive.

Do pick up on time so your child does not become anxious as other children leave.

Do tell your child if there is a change in your routine that will affect him. Let him know if you or his regular caregiver is not picking him up.

And Some Don'ts

Don't introduce anything else new in your child's life. This is not the time to make the switch from a crib to a bed or to introduce a

SURPRISING FEARS

You may be astonished, as you discuss the topic, at some of your child's expectations and concerns about school. Stories on television and in the movies, as well as tales from older children, can create questions or even anxiety in your child's mind. Some preschoolers believe that they will learn to read at school and wonder if they are up to the task. Others are concerned that they have to have a certain set of skills before they can attend. Sometimes, they hear youngsters on television or cartoon characters declare that they hate school. This can be confusing for a young child. He might think: Why should I like a place that other kids say they hate?

Sometimes you have to play detective to find out what's troubling your child about school. In one family, a little girl was starting preschool at the same time that her oldest brother was leaving for his freshman year at college. She had originally been very excited about starting school, but soon became very anxious whenever the topic came up for discussion. Finally, after careful quizzing by her parents, the little girl confessed that she was worried because she thought she would have to sleep at school just like her big brother!

You need to reassure your child that the purpose of preschool is to have fun and play—and that she will come home to you every day.

new sitter. Life should, as much as possible, remain constant while introducing your youngster to school.

Don't take away any security items. Wait until your child is comfortable in school before encouraging her to give up the pacifier or bottle.

Don't rush home from vacation just before school starts. Plan to be at home, in your usual routine, at least five days before the opening of school.

Don't let your child suspect your own concerns about his adjustment to preschool.

Four Weeks Before School Begins

Now is the time to read books together about going to school. You want a range of books: some that acknowledge a youngster's concerns; others that illustrate a typical day in preschool; still others that are just plain silly.

Talk about the books and what the characters are feeling. You want to listen to your child's questions and concerns. Discuss the differences between the school your child will attend, and the ones you find in the book. For example, after reading *The Berenstain Bears Go to School*, by Stan and Jan Berenstain, you could ask if your youngster thinks her teacher will be a bear like the one found in the story. It will probably produce a set of giggles from your little one, but the question also allows your youngster to make the connection that the schools described in books are similar, but not necessarily the same as the program she will attend. (See Suggested Reading.)

Two Weeks Before School Starts

Now is the time to start buying school supplies and clothes your child will need. You may want to do this together, but again, you need to judge your own child and her interest and ability.

Some youngsters enjoy a trip to the store and can make a decision (and live with it). For others, choosing among a dozen backpacks or lunch boxes is frustrating, and produces tears and wails of "why can't I have two backpacks?"

Check with your school for what you need, but here is a list of what most schools suggest.

Backpack It's hard for little hands to carry, without dropping or losing, the various items that make the trip to and from school each day. A backpack or tote bag simplifies life. In it you can stuff mittens, scarf, hat, etc., as well as favorite security objects that travel with your child on a daily basis. It can also hold a lunch box if necessary and, of course, any notes you may want to stick in, and any notices that need to come home. A backpack can also hold finished art projects—a rolled up painting can stick out the almost closed zipper.

Be sure and print your child's name in indelible ink on the outside of the backpack.

Lunch box If your child needs to bring a daily snack, or a lunch, you'll want to purchase a lunch box. Your child may enjoy picking one out. Again, print her name in indelible ink on both the lunch box and the thermos.

Smock To cover school clothes when painting, most schools ask students to bring in some kind of cover-up. You can buy a smock, but any old shirt (adult size) will do. Be sure and write the child's name on the cover-up. Because smocks get a lot of wear and tear during the course of the year, splattered with paint and other art materials, they may not survive from one class to another. Don't invest a lot of money in them.

A WORD ABOUT CLOTHES

A good preschool program is hard on clothes. **If it's not washable, you don't want it.** Despite wearing a cover-up when doing art projects, paint almost inevitably ends up on some part of the outfit.

> **TIP:** Where possible, don't get into an argument over clothes. Let your youngster pick out what he is comfortable wearing, even if it means plaids and stripes together. Their fashion sense will kick in later. The rule is: Clothes should be clean and weather sensible.

SOME PRESCHOOL FASHION TRICKS

✎ Put a happy face on the right shoe/boot to help your child when he puts on his shoes. (It also helps him learn right from left.) Alternatively, put two happy faces on the inset of each boot. When the faces are looking at each other, the boots are on correctly.

✎ Put plastic bags (the kind that come wrapped around the newspaper are perfect) inside your child's rubber boots to ease them on.

✎ Put a mark on the inside of underwear, shirts, pants, and sweatshirts to distinguish the front from the back. Be consistent so that your child will learn to recognize the mark as indicating the front (or back) of clothing items.

✎ Velcro is a blessing for preschoolers who want to dress themselves. They will learn to tie their shoes when they are developmentally ready. Let them enjoy the independence that velcro shoes gives them.

✎ Avoid reversible jackets because they are harder to zip. Buy coats with large commercial zippers as they are easier for preschoolers to manipulate.

✎ Choose pants with elastic waists. No buttons or zippers for preschoolers who frequently wait until the last minute to use the toilet.

✎ In a pinch, substitute socks for mittens/gloves.

The wear and tear on knees during playground time makes many parents sew on extra patches before the pants are worn. You want to buy durable, washable, comfortable clothing. The emphasis is on practical, clean, and weather sensible.

Children can get fixated on certain outfits, wanting to wear them every day. These clothes serve as a form of security blanket, easing the transition from home to school. One little girl wore the same sweatshirt every day for months. While her mother was initially embarrassed, the teacher reassured the parent that this was typical preschooler behavior. Another little boy refused to wear jeans, insisting he would wear only "soft pants."

> **TIP:** Keep your pre-opening day visit short and up-beat. Don't stay too long in the classroom—the teachers need the time to prepare for the opening days of school.

SET A SCHOOL NIGHT BEDTIME

Now is a good time to start becoming a little more strict about bedtime, if you haven't been previously. Preschoolers need about 10 to 12 hours a night sleep (in addition to a nap or rest period in the afternoon for the under-three set). You want them to be fresh and rested before a busy morning of preschool.

Establish a family schedule so that you avoid "morning crazies." Working backward from the time school opens, determine when you and your child must get up in order to get dressed, eat breakfast, and travel to school. Build time into the schedule for your youngster to "dawdle" (since that will inevitably happen). You want to avoid a morning rush so that your nerves are not frayed before the day even begins.

Another trick to cut down on the "morning crazies" is to set your own alarm clock for at least a half hour earlier so that you can be dressed and ready when your preschooler rises.

One Week Before School Starts

Go on a scouting mission. Now is the time to take a walk around the school building, try out the playground and, if possible, visit the classroom. Check out the bathroom and locate the cubbies.

In some schools, teachers visit each child at home before school begins. This is very helpful. It's also valuable, if possible, to meet your child's teacher in the classroom a few days before school. The informality of such a meeting is comforting, and it permits your youngster to visualize where she is going to be spending her mornings, and with whom.

What Does the School Need to Know?

Before school begins you will complete an information form about your child. This will help the staff make placement decisions and ease adjustment problems. Generally speaking, the more information you provide the staff about your child, the better they can help ease her adjustment to preschool. For example, if your child has already begun to read, loves dinosaurs, is afraid of bugs, it would help the staff to know.

BUT WHAT ABOUT PERSONAL FAMILY PROBLEMS?

On the one hand you want to protect your privacy, but it's rare that you can hide any family crises from your children, even if they are young. Divorce, legal problems, infertility, chronic or serious medical condition, they all take a strain on the parents that almost inevitably shows on the children. It's not that you're not doing your best to protect your child, but why not let the preschool staff help your child cope. If you have chosen a good preschool, the teachers see it as part of their job to help youngsters and their families.

ADOPTION

Some adoptive parents are hesitant to tell the preschool that their child is adopted because as one mother pointed out: "I don't want them to frame everything my daughter does in the context of 'she's adopted.'" This parent was concerned that the school would be looking for problems where none exist.

It's understandable to want to protect your child and resent any attempts to think that all adopted children are struggling with the issue. However, again assuming you have chosen a good preschool, you are probably doing your child a disservice if you don't tell her teachers that she is adopted. The topic may or may not come up for conversation, but in preschool there are frequently many siblings being born and the way families are made is a natural outgrowth of these births. Better that the teacher can frame the conversations that may ensue so your child feels comfortable.

Furthermore, if your youngster is raising questions in class about her adoption, it will help you to know.

WHEN THE TEACHER VISITS

When the teacher visits a child at home, it is an opportunity to meet in a familiar setting. Take your cues from the teacher on how the visit should progress. Generally, the conversation is primarily between the teacher and your child, although you or the caregiver should stay in the room. Don't feel like you have to fill in the silences or speak for your child.

Preschool teachers recognize that not all young children are comfortable talking, while others love to chat. It's not a reflection on your youngster or her future adjustment to school. The teacher may ask your child about her favorite activities. Perhaps your child will be asked to show off her beloved stuffed bunny.

This is not the time to bring up any concerns you may have. Ask, instead, if the teacher will call you or set up a time for a conference.

The Night Before

Get organized. You want to avoid minidisasters in the morning, so lay out what you and your child *both* agree she will wear in the morning. Again, the emphasis is on comfort, both physically and psychologically. If you have bought your youngster a new outfit for the first day of school, make sure to wash it to rid it of any stiffness. Similarly, make sure that new shoes are "broken in."

Most preschools ask families to bring in a shoebox/plastic bag with a full change of clothing (in case of "accidents").

If you have any additional paperwork you must provide the school, place it in an envelope with your child's name on the

---

TIP: Remember to update the clothing in the box during the school year to take into account growth spurts and change of season.

> **TIP:** Try to arrive early at school so that your child can begin to settle in before she is overwhelmed by the press of children.

outside, so that you can bring it with you in the morning. Put all school supplies by the door (and perhaps a camera for opening day photos) so that you don't have to search for last-minute items in the morning.

The First Morning

Build a few extra minutes into your schedule the first few days of school until you and your child get the morning routine down pat.

Even if your child is very excited (or nervous), try to encourage her to eat a balanced breakfast. Skip the sugar cereals and go for a nutritious meal that will provide her with a morning full of energy. But this is no time for a food fight. What you are trying to do is make the morning as easy and stress free as possible.

Separation Anxiety

WHAT IS IT?

You don't have to be a preschooler to suffer from separation anxiety. Consider how you would feel if you were asked to go into a room full of strangers, in a place you had never visited before (or only briefly). And suppose you couldn't tell time so you had no concept how long you would have to endure the experience. Wouldn't you welcome the sight of a friendly face? Wouldn't you want someone in the room you knew that you could always count on? Wouldn't it be nice to have someone with you who would offer reassurance, even if you did like this new, exciting place?

Separation anxiety is a normal part of childhood. It is not only developmentally appropriate, but actually essential, that pre-schoolers have a strong attachment to their parents. Research has shown that this same attachment, formed in the first year of a baby's life, is the foundation for a healthy emotional development in adults. The loving, trusting relationship that an infant develops with his parents teaches the child that the adult world can be counted on to provide him with his basic needs.

The flip side of attachment is, of course, separation. And that can be scary for a young child. But just as an infant learns that his mother will come from behind her hands and reappear when they play a game of peekaboo, it's part of a child's emotional development to learn to trust so that parents can leave and then return. A preschooler will discover that separation is followed by reunion. But for some perfectly normal children, the anxiety over the separation takes longer to relieve.

WHAT SEPARATION ANXIETY IS NOT

It's important not to measure your success as a parent by your child's adjustment to preschool. If your youngster falls apart when you try to leave the classroom, it doesn't mean that somehow you failed to create an independent child.

Nor should you wonder *why* the hysteria at your leaving the room. At times it's almost as if your youngster believes he will never see you again if you try to leave. As one father asked: "It's not like I've ever *not* picked her up or not returned when I've gone out. Why is my daughter so worried?" Another mother commented that she was offended that her son didn't seem to believe her when, trying to exit the classroom, she said she would just be in the next room having coffee with the other mothers. "I had never lied to him before. I had never left without telling him or sneaked out of the house when we had a sitter. So why didn't he believe me?" Of course, later on, when she had calmed down, this mother could recognize that she was looking for a logical response in a situation when her two-year-old just needed comfort, and couldn't respond to reason. Remember, when adults are very anxious, they don't always act logically or respond to reason either!

Separation anxiety in a preschooler is not about your child loving or trusting you enough. You do have a good relationship—in fact so good he doesn't want to risk it by having you leave. It's developmentally appropriate and, as with many childhood problems, this too will pass.

SO WHY ISN'T HE CRYING?

It's equally important not to feel upset or worried if your child sails through separation with nary a backward glance. It doesn't mean you failed to develop a strong attachment to your child, nor that she doesn't love you enough to care if you stay or leave. If your child handles separation well, enjoy it. One mother was slightly chagrined when she arrived at pick up time on the first day of preschool to hear her son wailing. She anxiously asked the teacher if he had cried the entire time. "Oh, no," the teacher instantly reassured her. "He only started crying when we told him it was time to go home!"

In the parenting worry sweepstakes, consider that you won on this issue, but there will probably be plenty of other occasions for you to worry!

WHO WILL CRY

Since separation is about change, it's not surprising that it affects some children more than others. You probably already know if your youngster adapts easily to change or is more likely to make a fuss in the opening days of school.

- ✎ How does he react to a new sitter?
- ✎ Does he readily try new foods?
- ✎ Is his bedtime routine fixed in cement?
- ✎ Is he shy around other children?

It's not that this type of child won't adjust to preschool, it's just that it may take a little more patience and reassurance as he adapts to this change in his life. Some children adjust to change more easily than others. It's not something to worry about, but it helps to be realistic about your child's general response to change.

Knowing that he often has problems adjusting to new situations allows you to plan your own schedule so that you (or your caregiver) are more available during the opening days of school.

Don't be afraid of crying. In many ways, it's preferable to deal with a child who is up front about his unhappiness and cries, rather than face the quiet child who retreats and is withdrawn. His unhappiness may be deeper and may be missed.

ON THE OTHER HAND

It's a fine line you walk. While you want to be prepared to help your child should he have a problem, you certainly don't want to act as if you expect a problem. If you hover too much, or overprepare your youngster, you may undermine your child's self-confidence. The message you may be sending is: "School is a place where you will be unhappy and you won't be able to cope with your sadness." You could end up creating a problem where one didn't exist. But this tightrope act is nothing new for parents!

YOUR CHILD'S AGE MAY AFFECT ADJUSTMENT

Separation tends to be more difficult at certain ages than others. Two-year-olds generally have more problems than threes and fours. This isn't surprising when you consider that a three-year-old has had more experience with separation from her parents and has learned that it isn't permanent. Age may also explain why some children in the class are having a harder time than others. If your child has a "late birthday," that is, he is one of the younger children in the class, you may notice that he has a more difficult time adjusting than some of his older classmates. Again, it's a perfectly age-appropriate response.

UNEXPECTED OR DELAYED PROBLEMS

Sometimes parents are surprised that their youngster is having trouble separating. She may have had a sitter since birth and never appeared troubled when Mom or Dad left. Remember that you are putting your child not only on "foreign" turf, but with a new set of adults. She has none of the "comforts" of home base. That is why carrying some security item with her to school can ease the transition.

Sometimes a child will enter school and for the first few days separate from her parents or caregiver with no problems. Then for some reason, she may begin to object when you leave the room. One little boy waved good-bye to his mother the first day, and effectively didn't look back as he entered the classroom. He was having a delightful time in school. Several weeks later, however, he started to cry bitterly each time his mother dropped him off. Why the change? Playing detective, his parents finally put all the pieces together and realized that the little boy's reaction was due to a combination of several factors: a classmate had knocked him down while arguing over a toy; his mother had recently given birth to a baby brother; his beloved grandfather was ill; and the family home was under construction. Was it any wonder that the preschooler was having a hard time separating?

Other times it's simply that the novelty of school has worn off and the child can now focus on separation. It's frustrating for parents, but generally these brief bouts of separation anxiety during the year pass quickly with the patience and reassurance of staff and parents.

AFTER HOLIDAYS OR ILLNESS

It's not unusual for a child to have problems separating after she has been away from school for several days following a holiday or illness. This is typical and can even occur after the weekend break. Again, reassurance and returning to the rituals you and your child have established will ease the anxiety.

PARENTAL SEPARATION ANXIETY

Sending your child off to preschool can be traumatic for parents as well. It can trigger an emotional response to think that babyhood, at least with this child, is behind you. One mother felt very

SCHEDULE FOR TRANSITION WEEKS FOR TWOS, THREES, FOURS

These are sample schedules for the opening days of school when the classes are phasing in. They do not reflect how long parents may be remaining in the classroom or within the school as their individual children adjust.

Two-Day Program for Two-Year-Olds

11 children in the class, three teachers

Meets Wednesdays and Fridays, from 9:15 to 11:30

The class is divided into Group I (six children) and Group II (five children)

September 11	Group I	9:15–10:15
	Group II	10:30–11:30
September 18	Group I	9:15–10:30
	Group II	10:45–12:00
September 20	Group I	9:15–10:30
	Group II	10:45–12:00
September 25	All Children	9:15–10:45
September 27	All Children	9:15–11:15
October 2	All Children	9:15–11:30

Three-Day Program for Three-Year-Olds

16 children in the class, three teachers

Meets Tuesday, Wednesday, and Friday from 9:00 to 12:00

The class is divided into two groups, each with 8 children.

September 11	Group I	9:00–10:15
	Group II	10:30–11:45
September 17	Group I	9:00–10:30
	Group II	10:40–12:10
September 18	All Children	9:00–11:00
September 20	All Children	9:00–11:30
September 24	All children	9:00–12:00

Five-Day Program for Three-Year-Olds

12 children in the class, two teachers

Meets five days a week from 9:00 to 12:00

The class is divided into two groups, each with six children

September 11	Group I	9:00–10:15
	Group II	10:30–11:45
September 12	Group I	9:00–10:30
	Group II	10:40–12:10
September 16	All Children	9:30–11:30
September 17	All Children	9:00–11:30
September 18	All Children	9:00–12:00

Five-Day Program for Four-Year-Olds

16 children in the class, two teachers

The class meets five mornings a week, from 9:00 to 12:00

The class is divided into two groups, each with eight children

September 11	Group I	9:00–10:30
	Group II	10:40–12:10
September 12	All Children	9:00–11:00
September 13	All Children	9:00–12:00

foolish when she came home from the first day of preschool for her youngest child and promptly burst into tears. For this woman, it was the end of one phase of parenting, and while there were still many years of family work ahead, there was sadness that there would no longer be a baby at home full time.

Children can be incredibly perceptive. Unconsciously, parents sometimes transfer their feelings of sadness or uncertainty about the preschool experience to their children. Watch those vibes.

THE OPENING WEEKS OF SCHOOL

You will receive a schedule from your child's preschool about the opening weeks of school. Some schools have a slower introduction to the full-time schedule than others. For example, depending upon the timing of the fall Jewish holidays, the full-time schedule of temple-affiliated preschools may be delayed until October or later.

How a school treats these transition weeks is important. It is an indication of their approach to children and you will want to be comfortable with the school's policy. Obviously you want your child to be with professionals who have coped with separation anxiety and can help your youngster adapt to this new situation.

Typically, for the first couple of classes, the teachers will divide the class in half and hold two abbreviated sessions. For example, during the opening days of a five-day program for three-year-olds, the class of 14 students will be divided into two groups of seven, each meeting for an hour for the first two days. Depending upon the progress of the students in separating from their parents/caregivers, the class might then meet as a whole group for a shortened period of time for the next three days (perhaps up to two hours), and then begin a full morning schedule the following week. That first week, parents may be invited to stay in the classroom until their child can effectively separate. Often there is a room nearby where parents/caregivers can go, perhaps for coffee, but still available to their child if needed.

WHO SHOULD ACCOMPANY THE CHILD TO SCHOOL?

For the opening days of school, it's most helpful to have the *same person*, preferably a parent, accompany the child. The child needs that kind of consistency. Once you know the timing for the first weeks, try to arrange your work schedule so that you can be available.

If the parents are unavailable, the child's regular baby-sitter or grandparent can substitute, but it should be someone with whom your child is very comfortable, **from whom your child can receive comfort**, and who agrees with your approach to dealing with your child's separation anxiety. What you want to avoid is having one person on day one, someone different on day two, and yet another person on day three.

The person accompanying the child should be the bedrock. When he is temporarily overwhelmed during those first days, your child must have someone to whom he can momentarily retreat, emotionally regroup, and then rejoin the class.

TRANSITION OBJECTS

Some children are fiercely attached to their blanket or a favorite stuffed animal. Tucking that security object into their backpacks can help ease the transition to school. Most schools will not permit children to bring pacifiers for health reasons.

Even if your youngster has never been particularly attached to a blanket or stuffed toy, he may find it helpful to bring an object from his room just to make the connection between home and school. These favorite objects also give a child the opening for a conversation with a teacher or fellow student.

Most schools forbid bringing any kind of play guns to school. Any toys that do come to school either must be shared with the class or limited to show and tell and then put away.

WHAT IF I AM THE ONLY PARENT LEFT?

It's hard not to compare your child to other youngsters—even if you intellectually understand that each child develops at her own pace. You sit on those child-sized chairs in the nursery-school classroom, as one by one other children have successfully separated from their parents/caregivers, and you may begin to wonder: "What's wrong with my child?" or "What have I done wrong?" The answer to both questions is most likely, "Nothing."

> **TIP:** If your child is going to bring a blanket or favorite stuffed animal, be sure to put his name on it. Your child needs to understand that the security object has to stay within the backpack or cubby since it's unfair to have a toy that all the children can't share. It also limits a child's mobility if he clutches the blanket/toy all morning.

You can't make your child walk any earlier than she is ready. So too you will find the issue of adjusting to school is not entirely within your control. Some children will do it in a day; for others it will take weeks—but all (or almost all) will do it eventually. Again, the parent-teacher partnership is critical to helping a child who is having trouble separating. If you are concerned:

✎ **Schedule a conference.** Ask the teacher if you can talk, either by phone or in person, *without your child present*, about your youngster's adjustment to school. The teacher can help put matters in perspective. She most certainly will reassure you that your child does not have the worse case of separation anxiety that she has ever seen.

✎ **Look for small improvements rather than quick cures.** If your child is having trouble separating, it's unlikely that one day he will suddenly turn and say "see you," (as nice as that scenario would be). Rather, acknowledge the small steps toward independence that he takes, and that at times, it may be two steps forward, one step back. For example, he may slowly become more comfortable playing with other children in the room, rather than clinging to your side, even though he may still require you to be available. Consider it a victory when you can move out of the classroom into the "coffee room."

✎ **Don't focus on crying.** Some children will continue to cry each time you leave even after they have adjusted to school. Sometimes, it is just a release of their tension about the concept of separating. They like school, but still fearfully anticipate the separation. In other cases, a child begins school with a separation problem and even when he is fully comfortable in school, he can't let go of the behavior. Discuss with your child's teacher how long the crying lasts—and how serious is your child's concern. The teacher may well reassure you that the tears are short-lived, and even more important, the child is quickly *and happily* engaged in another project.

✎ **Consider changing your routine.** While in some situations it's helpful to keep things as stable as possible, sometimes, a child separates more easily from one caregiver than another. For example, one mother discovered that there were no tears

TIPS TO EASE SEPARATION ANXIETY— PARENT TESTED!

Here are some additional tips that other families have used to ease the good-byes. Perhaps one, or a combination of several, will work well with your child.

1. Put a picture of your family in your child's backpack or lunch box. It's a tangible reminder he can look at during the day.
2. One mother kissed her daughter's hand each day and left a lipstick impression. Mommy's kiss could last the whole school day. Another mother put the kiss imprint on a tissue, which her daughter tucked into her pocket.
3. Be specific in terms your child can readily understand about when you are coming back. "I'll pick you up after snack and story time" is more easily understood by a preschooler than saying you'll be back in two hours.
4. Send a note with your child on a small piece of paper that can be slipped into his pocket. Make it simple ("I love you") or even a funny joke. Again, it's a tangible reminder for your child that you are thinking of him and he can be in "touch" with you. You can draw your message in pictures. If you think your child is comfortable talking to his teacher, reading the note is something the two of them can share. Add a "hello" to the teacher.
5. One child found it easier if she could shut the door behind her mother as she left the building. It made her feel as if she were sending her mother off to work.
6. One little boy needed to wave good-bye from the window just before his mother got in her car as a final step in separating.

when she said good-bye at home and allowed the baby-sitter to take her son to preschool. It wasn't a reflection on the parent-child relationship, but rather the little boy found it more comfortable to leave his mother, rather than she leave him.

ALWAYS SAY GOOD-BYE

This is the hard part because there are times when your child is completely absorbed in some activity, it's clear that you could leave and he'd never noticed, and all the experts are telling you that you have to interrupt him to say you are leaving, which will probably prompt a scene. Why always say good-bye?

Because **trust** is the foundation of the parent-child relationship. Your child has to know that he can count on you, that you won't trick him. If he looks up and you're not there, he will feel abandoned and will be more fearful the next time he goes somewhere new with you.

- ✎ **Make the good-bye warm, but brief.**   A kiss, a hug, and then walk out the door. If your child is having trouble separating, the teacher will help with the transition. She will comfort him and engage him in an activity.
- ✎ **Never ridicule or minimize your child's discomfort.**   Comments like "only babies cry" are hurtful and counterproductive.
- ✎ **Resist comparisons.**   While it may be frustrating if other children in the class are separating more easily than your own child, it doesn't help to point this out to your youngster. He can't help the way he is feeling. Do you want him making unfavorable comparisons between you and other parents? Focus on what you and he can do to make the good-byes easier.
- ✎ **Establish a routine.**   Whatever your special good-bye ritual will be, repeat it on a daily basis. One mother said good-bye with the phrase: "See you later, alligator," to which her daughter replied: "After a while, crocodile." Simple, but effective. Going through the ritual helps your child make the transition from you to school.

WHAT IF YOU DISAGREE WITH THE TEACHER?

If your teacher thinks that your child is ready for you to leave the classroom—but you don't—it's time for a conference. You both need to express your reasons for the decision. You may be seeing problems in your child's behavior at home that the teacher needs to know about. Conversely, the teacher, from her experience with other preschoolers, may be able to reassure you that your child is ready, even if he stills appears tentative.

Talk about the pattern of your child's reaction when you have tried to leave and how the teacher will comfort him and ease the transition. After discussing the matter, make a decision, **but agree to review it within a week (or sooner if it's obvious that there has been a significant change in your child's behavior).**

To a certain extent, you need to trust the teacher's judgment. On the other hand, and this is important to remember throughout your child's school career, you are his parent and there will be times when you need to trust your own instincts.

Remember, the separation issue is not about whether you or your caregiver has a few extra hours in the morning, or whether the classroom is crowded with an extra adult in the room. **Being able to successfully separate from his parents will boost your child's self-esteem.** It is the foundation of the preschool curriculum.

WHAT IF IT REALLY ISN'T WORKING OR "I HATE TO GO TO SCHOOL"?

Suppose it is now months after school has opened and your child is still clearly unhappy and uninvolved in the program. The morning refrain is always "I hate to go to school." The teacher will probably approach you and ask for a conference; if not you need to set up an appointment.

It's hard not to take it personally, but remember that it is your child's happiness that is the issue in this discussion. There may be several reasons why it's not working out.

IS SHE READY FOR THE CLASS SHE IS IN?

One little girl, with a December 26 birthday, was enrolled in a three-year-olds class when she was two and nine months. She cried bitterly each and every morning, and could not be coaxed into participating in class activities. She was not fully toilet trained and her speech and motor skills were clearly behind most of her classmates. Technically, she was eligible for this class (the cutoff date for birthdays was December 31), but the program was doing her no good, and perhaps some harm. The parents and teachers decided to move the little girl into the two-year-olds class where she flourished.

IS HE READY FOR PRESCHOOL?

Another child, a boy whose birthday was in July, also had a tough time adjusting to the two-year-olds class. Although he was two when the class began in September, he was unhappy and uninvolved. The teachers recommended, and the parents agreed, to withdraw from the program. The following year, the little boy happily and successfully began in the three-year-olds class. He needed the time to develop.

If the concept of a nursery school dropout seems daunting, it's important to keep things in perspective. You are doing what is best for your child at this time.

IS IT A BAD MATCH?

It's also possible that the school and your child are mismatched. One family discovered that withdrawing their child from a large preschool (class size was 15, with two teachers and total enrollment of the preschool was over 100) and enrolling her in a smaller program was just the answer. There was nothing fundamentally wrong with the first school, but it was too overwhelming for their three-year-old. The number of children was daunting. She skipped into class in the new program, which had only eight children in the class and two teachers.

Questions and Answers

Q: My son loves his Spiderman pajamas and insists on wearing the top and a pair of red boots (he switches the bottoms for a pair of Superman underpants worn under his jeans) on the first day of school. Should I insist that the outfit is for nighttime use only?

A: Clothing wars are generally a no-win battle for parents. When possible, permit your child to pick out his own clothing as long as it's clean and weather sensible. Even if he insists on boots during the summer. This won't hurt him. On the other hand, it is also reasonable to insist on your child dressing in appropriate clothing for certain occasions, for example, when he attends church/synagogue. Just as kids learn that you have to be quiet in the library, that there are places where you have to use your "indoor voice" rather than your "outdoor voice," they also learn that there are times that the Spiderman pajamas just won't do.

Some schools (often Montessori programs) do not permit students to wear clothes with "fantasy" characters imprinted. They believe it limits a child's imaginative play to repeating cartoon scripts or encourages "violent" play (e.g., pretend karate chops, etc.). In that case, you might suggest that your son wear the Spiderman shirt as an undershirt, so he still has it with him, but it is covered.

Q: **My 21-month-old daughter is very attached to her "binky" (pacifier). She will be starting a two-day preschool program in the fall. Can she take her "binky" to school?**

A: Preferably not. It's not that preschools are against security objects, they're very helpful to smooth the transition to school. But a pacifier can limit your daughter's speech and can get dirty, dropped, or lost in the preschool confusion. Several months before school begins, try to limit the pacifier to "at home" use only, and then, if possible, to give it up completely. If your daughter is resistant, make a deal that the "binky" is for bedtime. One mother found that her three-year-old daughter readily accepted that her "binky" was for bedtime only, but needed to have the pacifier on her bureau during the day. She never actually uses it, but the fact that it is within reach, gives the little girl a sense of control. Your daughter may find it difficult the first day or two when she doesn't have her "binky" for constant use, but generally it's not that hard to give it up. Praise her in the evenings when she has gone through the day without the "binky," but never scold or ridicule her when she needs it.

Q: My son is almost three and still not toilet trained. Should we still enroll him in preschool this fall or wait a few more months until he is wearing "big boy" underpants?

A: Most preschools don't expect all children in the three-year-olds class to be toilet trained. In one four-year-olds class, half of the boys were still not trained until December. And certainly "accidents" are routine in a preschool day. Talk to your child's teachers about how they encourage and reinforce the "newly" or "in the process of being" toilet trained. Again, at home and at pick up time after school, praise for the successes, reassurance when there are "accidents."

Q: My three-year-old daughter doesn't seem to be adjusting to preschool. She refuses to let me leave the classroom. All the other parents have been out of the classroom for more than two weeks. I like the teachers and the program, but am confused if I am supporting my daughter when she really needs me by staying with her—or spoiling her by not insisting that she learn to cope. The teachers want me to give it some more time, but should I?

A: Preschool teachers will be honest with you when they believe that your daughter is ready to make the transition. It's frustrating to be the last parent left in the room, but if you have the ability to stay, then you should. Just like some children say their first word at nine months, while for others it's 15 months, each child handles separation at their own pace. Look for small steps of improvement; moving from being in the classroom the entire morning to being able to leave the room for 15 minutes. Take it step by step, day by day, with the knowledge that sometimes you will be taking a step backward as well.

Ask for weekly conferences to see if both you and the preschool teachers agree on the strategy. If your daughter seems able to enjoy and participate in the program while you are there, then she is learning from the experience, even if it is not exactly what you had anticipated. In one school, although this was an extreme case, a mother stayed in the classroom the entire year. When her daughter entered the four-year-olds class the following September, she separated without a backward glance on the very first day. This was a case where the school and parents agreed to a strategy that worked for the little girl and her entire family.

5

WHAT'S HAPPENING
AT SCHOOL?

"**S**OS," short for "same old stuff," was the standard answer one preschooler gave to the perennial parent question: "What happened at school today?" The mother condensed the answer to the acronym, SOS, and the stock reply became a family joke.

Parental curiosity about their child's day in school is normal. Some families have a child who is a little chatterbox and will divulge the preschool day on a minute-by-minute basis. But most parents find their youngster's reply generally runs to the "I dunno," "nothing" or "I can't remember," variety.

But a good preschool class is a hub of activities that encourages the physical, emotional, social, and intellectual development of your child. There's an educational component in each part of the normal preschool day. Fun with a purpose. Whether it's sharing news during circle time, working on an art project, climbing, running, and biking on the playground, exploring nature, eating snacks, building with blocks, beating a drum during music, or cleaning the table, your child is learning new skills, refining and developing others.

Encouraging your child to tell you about her day at school is satisfying for both of you—and educational as well. Your child learns how to organize her thoughts and communicate them. You get an insight into your child's life away from you. Learning about the preschool day also allows the parent to build upon the skills that are learned at school.

But don't underestimate the importance of privacy for preschoolers. While you want to be able to talk about her day, your child, just like an adult, is entitled to keep some parts of her life private. Parents must learn ways to encourage a conversation without subjecting their child to the "third degree."

As with much of parenting—it's a fine line.

What Happens at School—and Why

A well-run preschool program looks deceptively easy. The children enter, perhaps chat for a few minutes in a teacher-led group, and then move into a morning full of activities. But there is a wealth of planning that goes into making each day a rich experience for the children. By understanding what goes on during a preschool day—*and why*, parents can more easily discuss with their child "what happened at school today."

In a well-organized program, the preschool class moves along seamlessly without abrupt transitions between activities. A good teacher prepares her students so that the change from one project to another, from one location to the next, is never jarring. There is a routine to the day, which is vitally important to young children who thrive in a consistent environment.

Part of the curriculum is built around units such as the holidays, the seasons, and national events. For example, during the presidential elections, the students in the four-year-olds class at one school, painted a voting booth (a large appliance box), could identify the presidential and vice presidential candidates, voted, and counted the results. The typical preschool curriculum also focuses on basic concepts such as family, weather, animals, and plants.

An equally valuable learning tool is a period of free play, when children can elect an activity in which they want to engage, whether it's art projects, painting, block building, housekeeping, water table, books, puzzles, games, clay, etc. Youngsters begin to understand about choice and self-control. They may need to learn patience as they wait their turn at the easel, playing with something else until it's their chance to paint. But they also are learning to respect others, to share, to communicate their preferences, and to socialize. Giving a child the option of which activity to pursue fosters her self-esteem and independence.

What Are *Prereading* and *Premath* Skills?

Educators often refer to the prereading or premath skills that a child will learn through play. These are the foundations on which a child will build competency in reading and math.

Children need abstract thinking in order to make the intellectual leap that words on a page represent ideas. As a child learns to express herself through art projects, telling stories, participating in dramatic play, she begins to understand that expressing ideas can be done in a variety of mediums, including the words on a page.

Similarly, many children enter preschool able to count to 10, 20, maybe even 100. But counting by rote is not the same thing as understanding that numerals are symbols for numbers. As children play with toys, they can classify, compare, measure, and order. As a preschooler helping to prepare snack for his class puts out one napkin for each student, he begins to make the connection between the numbers he can rattle off and the concrete numbers that correspond to napkins.

There is an educational component to the myriad of activities in the classroom. Many are subtle and slowly build upon the knowledge the child is gaining each day she is in the program.

Program Structure

The preschool day should be organized to recognize the needs and interests of young children. Free play and playground time should be scheduled for longer blocks of time (up to an hour each) because preschoolers can become absorbed in an activity and should have the opportunity to focus on it for an extended period. Free play and playground time also give children the opportunity to move around

A TYPICAL DAY AT PRESCHOOL

9:00–9:45—Free Play

Children arrive at school. After taking off their coats, they begin a period of self-selected structured free play. Children may choose any of the activity corners (housekeeping, art, books, blocks, puzzles, games, etc.). There may also be a project for that day that the teachers will have ready for those who want to participate. This could be a class mural about the season, a thank-you poster to the dentist who visited the class, individual hand puppets made from socks, etc.

9:45–10:15 Circle Time

After cleanup from free play, teachers and children sit together to talk. Teachers may use this time to discuss a specific theme (for example, seasons, holiday, name recognition of each class member). This is also an opportunity for the students to share with the class. For example, a child might show a favorite toy or tell of a recent experience, such as a trip to the zoo. Teachers often use circle time to sing songs with the children, lead a "marching band," or do some creative movement exercises together. It's also an opportunity to teach finger games (for example, the hand movements that accompany the song "Five Little Monkeys").

10:15–10:40 Snack Time

While the snack is being prepared by the teachers (with student helpers to set the table), the children may be encouraged to look quietly at books. During snack time, the teacher may also read to the students.

10:40–10:55 Toilet and Coats

11:00–11:30 Playground

Children may choose self-selected activities outside. This might be running, climbing, biking (feet propelled for younger children), playing imaginative games, digging in the sand, etc.

Alternatively, after snack, the class may do a group project between 10:40 and 11:10, and then go outside to play until dismissal.

11:30 Dismissal

to different activity centers when interest in any one thing begins to diminish. Furthermore, children develop complex thinking skills when they have the time to fully explore an experience.

The program should reflect a balance between active and quiet activities. Young children have a lot of energy, but also tire easily. The preschool program should build in both time to run around and time to sit and listen to a story.

Young children are not very good at waiting. The daily schedule should minimize the amount of time a child is sitting waiting for the next activity to begin. Many teachers, for example, sing songs or play finger games as children sit by their cubbies at pick up time. At other schools where circle time or a structured activity is first thing in the day, teachers will have puzzles, games, Play-Doh, or art supplies out for the children who arrive early so they have something to do while the rest of the class arrives.

On the other hand, the time when young children are in a group, such as story time or circle time, should be shorter (generally less than 15 minutes) because it's difficult for a young child to sit for too long. That's why a teacher might include some creative movement activities as part of circle time so that the children can get up and move.

How the day is organized is also a reflection of the teacher's preferences and practical considerations. A teacher may choose to begin the day with a brief circle time to help organize the children for the morning's activities. She may hold another, longer circle time later in the day to read together or have some other group activity. Depending upon the availability of playground space, the school may have to schedule playground time among the classes throughout the morning, with some classes going out first thing in the morning and others later in the day.

Transitions

Transitions are the in-between periods when children are moving from one activity to another. They are critical to the smooth running of the class day. Some children have difficulty shifting gears and strongly resist moving to the next activity. A good preschool teacher develops a routine so that the students know what to expect and have plenty of warning when one activity will end. For example, one teacher of three-year-olds made up a jingle (using a tune from a commercial) that she sang at the end of free play each day. "Five more minutes left to play, then we put the toys away." The children quickly learned that signal indicated that cleanup time would soon begin, followed by snack, and then playground time. The warning signal also gives the children time to finish what they are doing.

It's also helpful for children to participate in the transitional activity. Young children want to be able to do things for themselves. When they know what comes next, first they help clean up, then the class goes to the playground, a child feels more in control and part of the decision-making process.

Routines

Predictability is essential for children—at home and at school. In a world over which they have little control, it is reassuring to children to know they can count on certain routines/structures/pre-dictability in parts of their lives. Parents quickly learn how important bedtime routines are to a good night's sleep—and how disruptive it is to a child when that routine is altered.

Similarly, children enjoy the predictability of a preschool day. They count on following the day's schedule—and knowing what is expected of them, and when. That's not to say that any given schedule can't be altered to fit the demands of the day. Surprise is also fun. But in general, one of the first things a teacher tries to establish is the routine of the day. Young children develop a sense of trust when they can predict what comes next.

On the other hand, as one teacher pointed out: "Sometimes a project is going so well that we extend the time we've allotted for it and cut back somewhere else in the day. During a beautiful fall morning, when the kids are actively engaged on the playground, we'll extend outside time for another 10 minutes and then cut back on circle time or read only one book instead of two during story time."

What Are Children *Learning* When They Play

Circle Time

Generally teachers begin this group time with a specific topic for discussion. It may be a topic related to a project the class is working on, or it may focus on a specific skill. For example, in the beginning of the year, the teacher may play games to help the children learn the names of each of their classmates. Students may also use the time for "show and tell." Teachers often also include music appreciation, group sings, and creative movement during circle time.

Some teachers hold circle time first thing in the morning as a way of organizing the class and the morning activities.

What's Learned These "chats" are an opportunity for the youngsters to learn how to organize their thoughts. As they talk about their experiences, children learn how to tell a story with a beginning, middle, and end. When a child learns the words to "The Itsy Bitsy Spider" or "I Know an Old Lady Who Swallowed a Fly," this is an important part of a child's informal education. This is "shared knowledge"—that is information that society assumes you know. For example, other children assume you know the words to familiar folk songs.

Music Appreciation/Creative Movement

Children enjoy both listening to music and making their own. Whether it's a group sing-along, marching in a percussion band, playing a triangle, or making up new lyrics to old favorite tunes, music is the universal language. Creative movement, learning to move your body through space, in time to the music or while pretending to be a falling leaf, is a creative way to tap into a child's imagination and artistic side.

What's Learned Music helps children connect the outer world of movement and sound with the inner world of feelings and observations. Playing games or moving to music is a powerful first experience in the artistic process. Children learn music the same way they learn language—by listening and imitating.

Finger play promotes language development, fine-motor skills, and coordination, as well as self-esteem. Young children are proud when they sing a song and can do the accompanying finger movements.

Listening to music also teaches important prereading skills. As youngsters use small drums or other percussion instruments (homemade or store-bought), they can play the rhythmic pattern of words. They can learn to hear the differences between fast and slow, loud and soft, one at a time and together, etc. When they try new instruments, they notice how each variation changes the music.

Creative movement expands a child's imagination. It's also a fun method of physical fitness—an important goal of child development.

Art Projects

Some art projects are part of a theme that the class is studying. For example, as part of the seasons' curriculum, the children might gather pine cones, leaves, and acorns during a fall nature walk. They will later use them in art projects, such as to make leaf rubbings, to assemble in collages, or to use as decorations for picture frames.

A good art corner will be stocked with materials that can be used in a variety of ways for projects. There should also be easels for painting individually (although sometimes two children will work at the same easel to create a painting together).

What's Learned A good art project teaches a child that his creativity is limited only by his own imagination. By transforming everyday objects, such as empty paper towel rolls and egg cartons into sculptures, imaginary bugs, or spyglasses, a child discovers that he can create a world of play.

Using materials in an art project reinforces and expands on the information a child has already learned in other contexts. For example, let's assume that the art project of the day is to make rubbings of leaves collected during a nature walk the day before.

If from a pile on the table, the child selects a dry leaf that crumbles easily, the youngster learns, in a concrete way, about life cycles in nature. Through trial and error, just like the scientist in a lab, the student might find that green leaves or shiny leaves hold up better for this art project.

Another art project might have the youngsters create a fall mural by pasting leaves, pine cones, and acorns on a large roll of paper. They might organize the project by sorting and classifying the leaves, by color, shape, and size. These are prereading and premath skills—as well as fun. In this same project, the group also learns social skills such as cooperative and group dynamics. Do the three-year-olds know this as they happily create a fall mural—probably not, but their teachers certainly do.

Art projects are also excellent for developing a child's fine-motor skills. It takes small-muscle control in order to manipulate clay, cut with scissors, paint with a brush, and color with markers or crayons. As these skills are practiced, they help a child gain mastery to cut with a knife, button his own shirt, and print his name.

Art projects build a child's self-esteem. The finished product, on display on the refrigerator, validates a child's sense of worth. It's another opportunity for a child to say "I can do it!"

The process, not the product, is the most important element of preschool art projects.

Outdoor Play

Running, swinging, climbing, jumping, hopping, biking, digging in the sand—outdoor fun is one of the favorite parts of any young child's day. A good preschool playground will have enough space and sturdy equipment that a child can use his imagination while exercising. For example, the jungle gym structure might have connecting slides, firefighter poles to shimmy down and then inch up, tunnels to crawl through, a swinging bridge that connects one side of the apparatus to the other. A child will use multiple skills and create dozens of scenarios as he plays on this one structure. There should be equipment for digging, hauling, building, and riding.

What's Learned Outdoor play refines a child's gross-motor (large-muscle) skills. The cross-lateral movement (right arm/left leg and vice versa) involved is critical to a child's later success in reading and writing. Playground time is also an opportunity to explore and manipulate a different environment.

Youngsters also love outdoor play because they can let loose their imaginations while getting physical. They can turn the jungle gym into a rocket ship, a castle, a firehouse—anything they choose.

Cooking

Children enjoy cooking. Sometimes they like the product, but even if they don't, they always appreciate the process. It's fun to do something that is a grown-up activity—and discover that kids can do it too!

Preschools often tie cooking projects to other themes the class is working on. For example, in the fall, a class may take a pumpkin and use it in a variety of ways. For a large pumpkin, the class may first decorate it with markers and use the pumpkin as a centerpiece on the classroom table. Later, the teacher will cut open the pumpkin and the students can estimate how many seeds are in the pumpkin. Later the class can count the seeds and compare the total to the estimates. The class can also roast the pumpkin seeds for snack, and finally bake pumpkin bread.

What's Learned Since cooking is a basic life skill, it fosters a child's sense of competence and independence when he can do it. Math skills are also an important part of the process as the cook needs to count and measure the ingredients. Cooking also refines small-motor skills as a child stirs, dices, and adds ingredients. It also teaches about nutrition—foods that are good for you and help you grow.

A child also discovers how things change if you alter the environment: liquid batter becomes a cake when baked; juice cups become popsicles when frozen. Cooking also helps a child's reasoning ability. He learns cause and effect. "If I don't put the juice cups in the freezer, they won't become popsicles."

Snack Time

What do you remember as the highlight of your own school day—lunch time and recess? It's not all that different for preschoolers.

Snack time is an important part of the preschool experience. Whether the food is provided by the school, or on a rotating basis by the parents, or cooked by the students themselves, snack time—just like mealtime in your own home—is an opportunity to "break bread," share, and communicate. The snack is usually simple, crackers or a piece of fruit and juice.

Snack time can also be an opportunity for children to try new foods. One little boy brought in the usual graham crackers and apple juice for the class snack, but also brought in his personal favorite—green olives. Surprisingly, several of the children were willing to taste the new delicacy!

What's Learned   Snack time is an opportunity for a child to learn social skills as she chats with her friend in the seat next to her. Passing out the snack and distributing a napkin and cup to each child teaches one-to-one correspondence and counting skills. Pouring the juice from a small pitcher to an individual cup requires small-motor control. Cleanup time after snack is another educational opportunity. Again, a child's sense of competence and independence are reinforced. Snack time is also an opportunity for a child to associate mealtime with pleasant feelings.

Free-Play Activities

Free play sounds vague, but is very much a planned activity. The child has the freedom to choose among many different activities, but the teacher has created the classroom environment and arranged the choices the child will find. Free play is not time off for the teacher. On the contrary, she should be paying close attention to the children, interacting with them, offering guidance and help where necessary, noting progress and difficulties.

Here are some of the activities that a child may choose during the free-play period.

Building with Blocks

There's so much going on in the block corner that it's easy to understand why it is often the most popular area in the preschool classroom. It can also become the focus of incredible territorial struggles. Sometimes groups of children begin to act as if they own the space. Often boys dominate the area, making it difficult for girls (or boys who aren't members of the block clique) to enter. One study suggests that if a teacher positions herself in the block corner for part of the day, girls are more likely to enter and use the area.

Building with blocks is lots of fun—and it teaches many skills that children will use later. One study indicates that many of the concepts learned from block building are the foundation for more advanced science comprehension. For example, a child learns about gravity, stability, weight, balance, and systems from building with blocks. Through trial and error, she learns inductive thinking, discovery, the properties of matter, and the interaction of forces. One researcher suggested that one reason you see fewer girls in advanced placement physics classes in high school is because they are excluded (intentionally or unintentionally) from many of the "play" activities that build scientific framework.

What's Learned   Blocks help children learn scientific, mathematical, art, social studies, and language concepts; use small-motor skills; and foster competence and self-esteem. Building with blocks also teaches life skills. Just putting away your groceries in the cupboard is using the same concepts of spatial relations, stability, and balance that you learned in the block corner.

Besides the scientific concepts discussed in the previous paragraph, blocks also are important in developing math skills. A child learns about depth, width, height, length, measurement, volume, area, classification, shape, symmetry, mapping, equality (same as), and inequality (more than, less than)—all from building with blocks.

Building with blocks also teaches art concepts such as patterns, symmetry, and balance. A child learns about symbolic representation, interdependence of people, mapping, grids, patterns, people and their work. A child gains prereading skills such as shape recognition, differentiation of shapes, size relations.

Language is enhanced as children talk about how to build, what they built, what is its function or ask questions about concepts or directions. And dramatic play is also a part of block building as children create stories to go along with their constructions.

Finally, building with blocks fosters a feeling of competence, teaches cooperation and respect for the work of others, encourages autonomy and initiative.

It's not just building with blocks that is educational—so is cleanup. Sorting and storing blocks teaches classification and one-to-one correspondence, which are important math skills.

Dramatic Play

The housekeeping/dress-up corner should be stocked with play items and props that encourage young children to play make-believe. Look for pots and pans, stuffed animals, dolls (soft, unbreakable, washable, and multiethnic), toy telephones, hats, purses and tote bags, unbreakable tea sets, doll beds and carriages.

What's Learned   Playing make-believe lets a child bring the complicated grown-up world down to size. Research demonstrates that children who are active in pretend play are usually more joyful and cooperative, more willing to share and take turns, and have larger vocabularies than children who are less imaginative.

Imaginative play helps youngsters to concentrate, to be attentive, and to use self-control. Think about how a child develops a game of supermarket. He must first set up the counter, put out the pretend cans of food, invite friends to shop, use the "cash register," and bag the groceries. All of these actions help a child to learn about sequential acts. He also has a story or script in mind that helps him to perform each of these steps in a logical and orderly way.

When children pretend they also learn to be flexible, substituting objects for those they do not have. For example, a child will use an empty paper towel roll for a telescope.

Through imaginative play, children learn empathy for others. Children will often act out a whole range of emotions when playing pretend, offering sympathy for a stuffed "doggie" that is hurt or for a doll that fell off a chair. We watch them scold a puppet for being naughty or tell a doll how proud they are because she used the potty.

Dramatic play encourages children to think abstractly, which is an important prereading skill. Children come to understand that words represent ideas.

Manipulative Toys

Children enjoy playing with a variety of toys that helps develop their fine-motor control. These toys include Legos, Bristle Blocks, Play-Doh, Peg-Boards, large beads to thread, and stacking and nesting materials.

What's Learned Manipulative toys help develop a child's fine-motor skills, which is a precursor to being able to write. Often these toys are also used in fantasy play. The beads that are strung become the necklace for the "queen" to wear. The Play-Doh creations include cookies for the impromptu "tea party."

Cooperative Play

During the preschool day, you should see children who are playing by themselves, but you should also see cooperative play, small groups or even the class as a whole working on a project. The amount of cooperative play increases as the children grow older. Some of this play may be child initiated, and some may be teacher directed.

What's Learned Working together, whether it's on a block building or planning a tea party, helps children to learn to respect the ideas of others. They develop their social skills, and social competence is an underlying goal of early childhood education. Children in cooperative play learn to contribute to joint efforts. They also learn how to problem solve by working together to find a solution.

Sand/Water Table

Sometimes the rubber basin is filled with sand (some schools use rice or grits, which are less likely to get into a preschooler's eyes), and it's almost an indoor mini-playground. Even children who don't ordinarily dig in the sand at the beach will find it fun to measure, sift, and pour the sand from one container to another. When it's filled with water, the basin becomes a doll bathtub or a sink for toy china.

What's Learned A child has a practical math lesson in fractions when she pours a cup full of sand into a two-cup container. It explains the concept faster and more clearly than a detailed discussion or drawing. Her fine-motor skills are also being developed as she washes a tea set or maneuvers a cup full of sand into a sifter. Her eye-hand coordination is helped.

As anyone who has sat on a beach knows, sand and water play is soothing. It encourages children to explore and learn about cause and effect. (For example, what happens if I put a sponge in the water? What happens if I then squeeze the sponge?).

There is no right or wrong way to play with sand and water (except to throw it out of the basin), so each child experiences success.

Puzzles

The classroom should have puzzles that vary in complexity, five-piece puzzles, as well as 12-piece puzzles, and puzzles made of different materials. You should also find puzzles that interlock and those that have individual slots for pieces (for example, a five-piece puzzle of five individual animals).

What's Learned Puzzles require abstract thinking: the ability to see a space and envision what belongs there. Puzzles also require fine-motor control in order to place the pieces into place. Having puzzles for varied skill levels permits children at all stages of development to experience success.

Books

The book corner should have books reflecting a range of levels. There should be simple board books, as well as picture books with a story line. The area should be comfortable, carpeted, and perhaps lined with pillows. It should be a place where a young child can go and look through books by himself—as well as a meeting place for story time for the class.

What's Learned   Children learn language skills from books. Whether they are looking at a book individually, or being read to as part of a group, when you make books a part of a young child's day you set the stage for a lifelong interest in reading.

Cleanup

Preschoolers don't yet know that grown-ups consider cleaning a nuisance. For them, it's another fun activity. It's not a question of efficiency. It's tempting sometimes for grown-ups to do the task themselves, rather than exercise the patience it requires to help a preschooler through a chore. But allowing the young child to put away the blocks, wipe down the tables, and put the toys back on the shelves is a valuable educational exercise.

What's Learned   Preschoolers learn to sort, classify, match, and organize when they put the toys back on the shelf. A good preschool classroom will have low shelves and individual bins for small toys, so that the young child can easily see where objects belong. The bins will be labeled (which helps develop language skills).

Preschoolers learn that helping behaviors and orderliness are valued. They see that it's important to take care of their environment—and that it's easier to find what you want when you put it back in its designated place. Cleaning up teaches self-discipline. Children learn how to follow simple directions. Working together as a class to clean up their room is another exercise in cooperation. As they work alongside their teacher and classmates, chatting and discussing the best way to approach the cleanup effort, language and social skills are being practiced. Preschoolers also enjoy feeling competent, independent, and responsible. With the instant feedback of a clean room and a job well done, a youngster's self-esteem is enhanced.

So What Did You Do in School Today?

Getting your child to talk about her day at school is important for everyone. It sets the tone for a family partnership in education. It tells your child that you are interested in what she does. It makes clear that, in your family, school is important.

But a child's reticence is a combination of factors.

✎ **Out of sight, out of mind.** A preschooler's ability to keep the memory of the day's events clear and in focus is different at this age. It's not that it wasn't fun or that it was so boring it wasn't worth remembering. Rather young children tend to focus on the here and now, rather than the past. *Where are we going for lunch? Who's coming over for a play date?* Those are their immediate concerns.

✎ **Language skills may be limited.** A preschooler's ability to organize his thoughts and communicate them clearly is still being developed in early childhood.

✎ **Too much to tell.** The preschool day is so chock-full of activities that it's hard for your child to single out one activity and talk about it. It helps if you understand the normal schedule so you can ask specific questions, which helps your child focus, for example: "What did you do during circle time today?"

✎ **Processing what's happening.** Sometimes young children (and adults too) need time to understand and incorporate an experience before they can talk about it. Don't be surprised that your child waits a day or even a few weeks before he talks about certain events. He needs the time to figure out what the experience means to him.

Let's Talk

So how can you improve communication with your child about school? Set the stage. It helps to have a block of uninterrupted time to talk about what's happening in your child's life. Turn off the television and put on the telephone answering machine. Snuggle down on the couch for a chat. It doesn't have to be too long—15 minutes is fine—but it tells your child that you are interested enough in his life to focus on him exclusively for a period of time.

Other parents find that doing a chore together with their child sparks conversation. As you both clean up the toys in the living room, your child may tell you about the cleanup routine in his classroom. Setting the table for dinner can be the perfect opening to ask about snack at school.

Riding in the car together is another opportunity for discussion. It's often a great chance for some quality one-on-one conversation.

Here are some other parent-tested tips that really work.

1. **Be specific.** It helps your child focus if you ask precise questions. For example, you could begin with "Who did you sit next to at snack today?"

2. **Get to know the kids.** Take the time to put the faces to the names your child is mentioning. Then you'll know whom she is referring to when she answers your questions and can keep the conversation going more easily.

3. **Familiarize yourself with the routine and layout of the classroom.** Understanding the daily schedule and knowing the activity centers in the classroom allows you to ask specific questions.

4. **Wait for an answer.** Don't be uncomfortable with silence. It may take your child a few moments to organize her thoughts about the day. Allowing time for her to answer your question helps develop her language skills as well.

5. **Be outrageous.** To break the ice you may want to suggest a silly scenario about what happened in preschool that day. For example, "I bet that you had green eggs and ham for snack today," or "Did an elephant visit your class this morning?" Once you get past the giggles, you might hear a more realistic explanation of the day's events.

DO THREE-YEARS-OLDS NEED PRIVACY?

You want your child to respect your privacy, and you must respect your child's need for privacy as well. Modeling behavior is always the most effective teaching method. For example, your child will learn to always knock before opening your closed bedroom door, if *you* always knock before entering her bedroom.

   If your child appears happy in school, does not exhibit any problems with sleeping, eating, socializing, etc., then you need to respect his willingness (and ability) to share his day with you on his terms. That may mean that some days he will be full of answers to the question: "What happened in school today?"—and sometimes he'll respond "SOS"—same old stuff and nothing more.

6. **Draw it.**   Your child might enjoy drawing a picture of his day more than just talking about it. After he completes his picture, let him dictate a caption of explanation.
7. **Model it.**   Talk to your child about *your* day over lunch or dinner. This shows her that discussing the day's events are part of your family's life.

   Crib notes.   Many schools send home a weekly calendar or "nursery-gram" that details some of the week's highlights and upcoming events. This can be a great help if you need some insight into what's happening in the classroom in order to spark the conversation. If your school doesn't provide this information, suggest it to your director. You might even offer to help compile, type, or copy the newsletter if the school is short staffed.

Friendships

Making new friends and keeping the old ones are some of the social skills your child is learning at school. That doesn't mean that every child is a social butterfly. Nor does it matter *how many* friends your child has. What's more important is that she is learning empathy and social interaction.

Twos and threes base most friendships more on logistics ("the child is here and willing to play") than on shared interests. Fours and fives begin to narrow down their choice of companions, but you will still hear about "best friends" moving in and out of favor with remarkable speed. By four, peer friendships are usually very important.

The teacher can be helpful in pairing up children during class projects to help youngsters begin to make connections. You should also ask the teacher for suggestions of children who might be good matches for play dates after school.

My Child Is Shy

Being shy shouldn't be considered a negative quality. To begin, it's often the case that a parent points out a child's shyness when the adult is also not very comfortable around strangers. Why should a child be any different?

Shyness is also typical behavior of most twos and threes. Of course, there is always the exception—the youngster who can walk up and charm any adult or child. That's terrific if you have one of those, but most children are shy at least some of the time.

Some children are very comfortable in the company of adults and less outgoing with their peers. That's frequently true of the firstborn or only child. And it's easy to understand because these children are frequently surrounded by adults and have fewer opportunities for peer interaction. Younger siblings are often the more outgoing, gregarious of the lot. Again, understandable. And research has shown that for about one in five children, the shyness is inborn rather than developmental. These children will tend to be shy even as they mature, although they can obviously work to overcome their natural tendencies.

No matter whether it's inborn or developmental, accept your child's personality and temperament.

✎ Reassure her when she is in social situations where she tends to hold back.

✎ Encourage friendships with less aggressive youngsters so she isn't easily overwhelmed.

130

✎ Help her break the ice by giving her suggestions of how to enter a group, for example, "Why don't you show Andrew your new truck."

✎ Ease her way into a group by joining her in her quest and then moving away once she has successfully entered the play. For example, you might ask some children who are building with blocks, "Can Erin and I help you build a garage?"

Suppose You Don't Like His Friends?

You can't always choose your child's friendships—which will become painfully obvious by the time he is a teenager. You also can't assume that just because you are friends with another mother, your child will like her offspring—and vice versa. You may not be able to stand certain individuals, but your children could become best friends.

But what do you do if your child has chosen a friend who doesn't seem to bring out the best in his behavior? The two of them tend to get more aggressive when they play with each other, get into more mischief, or your child seems to be picking up unacceptable habits or language.

First of all, your own family life will have a more long-lasting impact on your child's behavior than any one friend. While you may not like your youngster's behavior when he is with a certain child, in the long run, your child is learning basic values *from you*.

While you probably don't want to refuse to let your child play with this child, you can try to expand his social circle. Ask the teacher for suggestions of other children in his class who might be good matches. Invite these youngsters to your home for a play date and supervise the afternoon carefully to make sure it goes well. You want other children to see that your child can be a good, fun friend.

Also set the rules for behavior in your home. If the disruptive child comes for a play date, insist on both children following "house rules" while in your home. Also, for the time being, make sure the play dates are in your home, rather than the other child's, so you can supervise the behavior.

Questions and Answers

Q: At home, my daughter loves to build with blocks, Legos, etc., but she never seems to enter the block corner at school. When I ask her why, she just shrugs her shoulders. Is it odd that she avoids doing one of her favorite activities at school?

A: There could be several reasons for your daughter's decision not to play with blocks at school. If she elects to try new and different activities at school because she has the opportunity to play with blocks at home, then fine, in fact, good for her!

On the other hand, if she feels that she *can't* play with blocks because she's unwelcome in the block corner, then you'll have to ask the teacher to intervene. While leaving the classroom one morning, a mother overheard a four-year-old firmly announce to another little boy: "You can't play here, we're building and you can't play." A brief conversation with the teacher made the block corner more accessible to all children.

You want to be especially alert that the school—and students—are not stereotyping any activities based on gender. Reinforce your daughter's interest in block building—it's educational (as well as fun).

Q: My nephew is only four, but he has been playing with the family's computer since he was two and his preschool classroom has a computer as well. I like my daughter's school, but there is no computer in the classroom—and we don't have one at home. Are all the prereading skills in a regular classroom enough to make up the difference with those children who have played a variety of prereading games on the computer before they enter kindergarten?

A: We all want to give our children an educational edge. There is no question that computers can be a fun way to reinforce prereading skills. But there is absolutely no research to indicate that the absence of a computer either at home or in the preschool classroom limits or retards a child's ability to learn to read and do math.

Remember that there is a multitude of research studies that

shows that young children learn best **through their senses.** They explore and understand what they can see, hear, touch, taste, and smell. *They learn through doing.* Your child will learn how to read if she never touched a computer. It's not a question of trying to turn back time and pretend that the electronic age is not here. Computers can be a fun, useful tool for young children, but it's the hands-on activities in a good preschool program that lay the foundation for building good reading skills.

Q: **My son brought home a picture he had painted in school and I promptly put it on the refrigerator. He announced that he didn't want it there because he didn't like it. I thought I was right when I answered, "I like it because you did it." Should I have taken the picture down?**

A: It was fine to tell your son that you like something just because he did it, but, nonetheless, it would have been better if you had respected his wishes. Next time, take down the picture and then say: "Okay, why don't you make me a picture that you would like to put up." You want your child to take pride in his work—and one way is to *show him* your are proud of his efforts by putting them up for display.

But sometimes children bring home artwork because they love it and can't wait for it to go up on the refrigerator gallery—and sometimes artwork comes home just because the teacher sent it home.

Artwork is a great way to start a conversation with your preschooler, but be careful how you phrase your questions. Don't ask: "What is it?" Often the child doesn't know or can't remember what he was trying to paint at the time. Instead, ask: "How did you make this?" *You want to focus on the process, rather than the product.*

Q: **My husband and I were shopping for our daughter's fourth birthday and disagreed on the level of complexity of several puzzles we thought of buying. Should toys and puzzles be slightly more difficult than a child's developmental level so that it's more of a challenge or scaled to a child's current level so that she can succeed?**

A: Both. Children need to feel successful at what they do, so a good preschool classroom (and home) offers opportunity for success, but they also grow when they meet a challenge. Keep the easy puzzles, even those she has apparently outgrown. It's nice to be able to complete them quickly, and builds her self-esteem. Sometimes children make a game of seeing how fast they can do the easy puzzles.

But you also want to have one or two puzzles that are a challenge. It's okay to let her try them on her own, but don't hesitate to offer some strategies if she appears frustrated. Working together on a puzzle is a great family activity.

Work on ways to approach the problem (rather than trying to solve it for her). For example, ask her to separate into two piles, the "outside" pieces of the puzzle (those with at least one straight edge) and the "inside" pieces. Next you could separate the "inside" pieces by color. Breaking down the puzzle into manageable pieces may make it easier to put it back together. But if your daughter is too frustrated by the process, then put the puzzle away for a little while. She may not be ready for that level of complexity.

6

FORGING A PARTNERSHIP

The Parent-School Relationship

Your child may be the one attending class every day, but education is a family effort. Even if your time is limited, you must make time to involve yourself in your child's school, beginning in preschool and continuing through high school (if not college!).

Parental participation is vital for many reasons. Of course, on a very practical level, the school often needs your help to make the program work. Class trips, which enrich your child's experience, won't happen unless there are enough adults to supervise young children. Special class projects frequently need extra assistance to help little hands manipulate materials.

But even if you can't spend time in the classroom, you can volunteer to do what you can do—in the time you have. With each effort, you are sending a powerful message to your child: *Education is important to our entire family*. In fact, it's important enough that Mom and Dad *make time* in their schedule to help.

Parent-teacher conferences are another opportunity to forge a strong, cooperative relationship with the school. It's the perfect time to enjoy reveling in the progress of your child as interpreted by another adult and a chance to ask any questions or voice any concerns about your child. Preschool teachers are an excellent resource for questions about behavior and development—both in and out of school.

If Possible, Volunteer in the Classroom

Every quality preschool program should have an open-door policy concerning visits from parents. That means that you shouldn't have to make an appointment to stop by the classroom. On the other hand, parental visits can be disruptive to the flow of the day, so while you should be welcome if you visit, an open-door policy doesn't mean you move in! One of the goals of preschool is to help your child become more independent—and if you are constantly there, it slows the process.

But by volunteering, whether regularly, on an as-needed basis, or even just once a year, you have an opportunity to see your child in a school context. Of course, as you have already discovered, your child does not necessarily behave the same way when you are around as when you are absent. Don't be surprised if she is more clingy, more demanding of your attention, or less willing to interact with the other children.

But this is also a chance to observe the dynamics of your child's class. One mother, who had been hearing complaints from her daughter about a three-year-old bully on the playground, was surprised when she finally met the little boy. She discovered that he was at least two inches shorter and 10 pounds lighter than her daughter. While she knew that her child's frustration and fears were real, as the mother pointed out: "It helped me put the problem in perspective, both for myself and for my daughter. The playground bully, who upon retelling was taking on Goliath proportions, could now be reduced to a very human level."

And there is an intangible benefit from volunteering when needed. Teachers and school directors are human, and may well remember who stepped forward when the call for help was sounded. It may mean that they listen a little more closely when you ask for a favor, or request a special teacher.

Special Talents

Your child may be unimpressed with—or unaware of—what you do professionally or as a hobby, but schools are delighted when parents share their talents with the students. Doctors and dentists can talk to the children about the human body and teeth care; firefighters, postal workers, carpenters, can each discuss on a child's level—and show—what they do. One parent who collected model trains invited the class to visit his elaborate display. Be sure to tell your child's teacher if you are willing to share your knowledge and talent with the children.

Classroom Behavior

When you are in the classroom, even as a volunteer, remember to maintain a certain level of professionalism. Classroom etiquette requires:

- ✎ no favorites, except for your own child, of course.
- ✎ never ignoring a youngster because you don't know—or don't like—him.
- ✎ following the classroom rules.
- ✎ asking the teacher for help if there is a problem or a question of discipline.
- ✎ interacting with the children. Don't use the time to chat with another parent volunteer.
- ✎ never gossiping about any of the students or what you observed in the classroom.

What If You Have No Time

You may not be available to volunteer during school hours. But there are still many ways to be helpful. You could:

- ✎ make calls as part of a class telephone chain;
- ✎ volunteer to prepare a class/school newsletter;

✏️ head (or assist) a fund-raising effort;
✏️ paint or repair school equipment;
✏️ arrange a speaker for a parents' meeting.

If You Can't Be There

Before you enroll your child in a school, you'll want to know what expectations there may be about the extent of parent involvement. If your schedule as a family does not permit a weekly or monthly classroom commitment—and that is expected—then you may be in the wrong place. **The most important person you are trying to please is your child.** You don't want to embarrass him if every other youngster's parent is at an event and you're not. Ask, **in September,** if there are any specific dates during the school year when parents are expected and mark your calendar—**immediately!**

Generally speaking, with enough notice, almost all parents will rearrange their professional and private schedules in order to share a special event with their child. But what we sometimes forget is that it doesn't have to be a child's debut on Broadway *for the occasion to be important to the youngster.*

In one Jewish preschool, each parent was asked to make a twice a year commitment to come in on a Friday morning for one hour to help the class celebrate the Sabbath. As the teacher explained, with some frustration: "Many parents don't understand how excited and proud three-year-olds become when it's their turn to be the 'host' for the Sabbath. We'll work with any family to try and accommodate busy schedules, but the parents have to understand that it's important to their child that one of them—and it doesn't have to be the mother—shows up. At the very least, send a substitute. Sometimes that's a grandparent or a sitter that the child likes, and we're happy to make the family and child feel comfortable. But most of all, I would hope that the parents understand that it's the small moments—and there are lots of them during childhood—that are important in a young person's life."

But that doesn't mean you have to rearrange your entire life to keep up with a preschool schedule. *First of all, parent involvement means either mother or father.* This is not a 1950s sitcom where only mothers appear at school. Even if your school still calls them "class mothers," dads can and should fill the bill. In fact, one could make the case that a dad helping out at preschool is a good role model for young children and teaches about sharing parental responsibilities.

If neither Mom or Dad can be present, ask the teachers if a grandparent or baby-sitter can substitute. One grandmother volunteered at crafts day at her grandson's school. As she explained: "His parents are getting divorced and with the turmoil at home, I thought it would help if I came in."

What should you do if a parent and only a parent is expected and you absolutely can't be there? For example, one preschool holds an annual "Father's Day" where dads accompany their children for a shortened class schedule. It's held on a Sunday to insure a greater turnout. But one father had to be out of town that particular weekend. This family decided not to send a substitute (although an uncle had volunteered), and kept the child home. You have to decide what will make your child—and you—comfortable. Talk it over with your youngster and explain your decision to the teacher so that everyone can support your child if he is disappointed.

Will your child hold it permanently against you if you don't show up at a preschool event? He may remember it, but its impact will be minimal if you are sensitive to your youngster's feelings. It's one of the inevitable parental facts of life: show up at every event, cheer loudly, bake for every fund-raiser, and your child won't remember any of it. But the one time you miss, it seems that's what your child remembers!

School Conferences

Every preschool should have regularly scheduled parent-teacher conferences. It's an opportunity for both sides of the equation to talk, without interruption, about the progress and development of the student. So why do so many perfectly confident and competent parents quake at the thought of meeting with their three- or four-year-old child's teacher?

One mother finally put her finger on why she was worried. "At least in elementary school, there are some quantifiable grades in subjects, like math, English, history, etc. Here I feel like the conference is about personal characteristics, like self-confidence, shyness, independence—and if my child isn't doing well, it's my fault. I can't help thinking that it's me who's getting a report card on *my* parenting skills."

Of course, that's not really the purpose of preschool parent-teacher conferences, but many mothers and fathers enter the classroom, perch on the child-sized chairs, and interpret teacher comments as if they were receiving a grade in Parenting 101.

At the other end of the spectrum are parents who scoff at the necessity or value of preschool conferences. Some parents suggest that these preschool conferences are a waste of time. They argue that a meeting with a preschool teacher won't tell them anything they don't already know about their child.

Clearly, the answer lies somewhere in between. Preschool conferences can give you a window into your child's life that is beyond you. As parents quickly discover, almost all children behave differently with strangers than they do in the confines of their own home. How your child relates to his peers; how he interacts with other adults; how he handles stress; how independently he performs; what activities he enjoys and dislikes—the answers to these questions and more should emerge from your conference. The responses may surprise you as you discover new sides and interests of the little person you send off to school.

A Professional, Personalized Approach

You should expect that a teacher will conduct the conference in a professional manner. This doesn't mean a formal presentation, but rather that the teacher is ready (preferably with written notes) and prepared to talk about your child. She should be able to relate some vignettes about your youngster, and perhaps show you some artwork or a block building he has worked on.

The conference should be personalized. You are there to discuss your child, not for a generalized overview of preschool activities. The tone should be helpful and encouraging. Even if your child is having difficulty adjusting to school, the teacher should be able to point out some positive characteristics about your youngster and any progress, however small, he is making. As one teacher remarked: "I don't care if it's only commenting on how the child combs her hair, I have to find at least one positive thing to say about every child. Parents are entitled to that recognition." You want to know that the teacher sees a balanced view of your child and is not focusing exclusively on the problems.

Avoid going into a conference with preconceived ideas or judgments. Any negative attitudes can block open, honest communication. That's not to suggest that parents shouldn't go to a conference with their own list of questions and concerns, but rather that you are there to listen, as well as speak.

What a Conference Is Not

There shouldn't be any big surprises at a formal parent-teacher conference. If over the course of time a teacher has observed a serious problem with the child or has a question about behavior, she certainly shouldn't wait for the scheduled conferences to discuss it. Similarly, a parent who is concerned about what is happening in the classroom shouldn't hesitate to call and ask to speak to the teacher, either over the phone or in person.

PARENT PREPARATION FOR CONFERENCES

- ✎ Think about what you want to say and ask of the teacher—and make a few notes before the conference.
- ✎ Be a good listener. You may want to take notes during the conference if that helps.
- ✎ Ask questions about any suggestions or comments the teacher may have. Don't hesitate to ask for a follow-up conference if questions arise after you've had time to think about what was discussed at the conference.

If there has been a significant change in the child's life, for example, if the family is moving to a new house, a grandparent is seriously ill, a parent acquires a new job or becomes pregnant, don't wait to share the information with the teacher. Even if you think you are successfully hiding a stressful situation from your child, youngsters are amazingly perceptive and pick up adult "vibes." Let your child's teacher help your youngster cope with any changes. Don't wait for the parent-teacher conference to give the teacher this vital news.

Sometimes, adults don't realize that even seemingly insignificant changes can affect a child. Your *child saw a scary cartoon on television, you had a near-miss accident while driving your youngster to school, a grandparent is arriving for a visit*—any of these situations may affect how your child behaves in class. Do both your child and the teacher a favor and share the information as it happens.

The regularly scheduled parent-teacher conference is an opportunity to reinforce and expand upon knowledge you already have. Any crises should have been dealt with as they arose.

When and How Often

Let's make a distinction between the casual conversation you have with the preschool teacher when you pick up at the end of the day and a parent-teacher conference. The first should be no more than a general comment on the day, perhaps a funny anecdote, or if necessary, a request for an appointment to discuss a problem privately. Conversations at the door, in front of your child or other parents, are not the time or the place for anything serious. Should the teacher—or you—have an important message to convey, suggest a one-on-one meeting or telephone call. You need to keep in contact with your child's preschool teacher, but it's unfair to discuss anything important in a passing, quick conversation.

In contrast, every preschool should schedule at least two parent-teacher conferences each year, one in the fall and another in the spring. These *child-free* meetings should last about 15 to 20 minutes. Preschools should make every effort to arrange these conferences to meet the needs of working parents, and conversely parents need to make sure that attending a preschool conference is a priority in their lives.

Why Both Parents Should Attend

If possible, both parents should attend all school conferences, beginning in preschool. Of course, this is not always possible, but it's significant for several reasons.

First, it sends a powerful message to your child. It tells your youngster, at a very early age, that both parents value education. When both parents attend a conference, your child learns that his schooling is a priority, important enough to be included in both parents' schedules.

Second, when both parents attend a conference, it sends a similar message to the teacher. She will understand that this is a family that shares child-care responsibilities.

Finally, each parent can contribute a different perspective about their child. As parents quickly discover, children relate to each parent in an individual way, and having additional viewpoints gives a teacher a richer understanding of a child's life.

The Fall Conference

For the first-time student, the fall conference is an opportunity for the teacher and parents to discuss the progress the youngster has made in adjusting to school. If all is going well, it's reassuring—and gratifying—to hear that your child is enjoying the experience. For those children having a harder time, teachers can offer a welcome perspective on the progress you, as a parent, may not recognize. Furthermore, a teacher can usually provide parents with the reassurance that as terrible as you think your child's separation process has been, they've seen worse!

At the fall conference you will want to ask:

1. What activities does my child like? What activities does she avoid?
2. How is she interacting with the other children in the class? Remember that young twos, threes, even fours, still do a lot of

parallel play. It's not a sign of maladjustment if she is playing happily alongside of, rather than with, another child.

3. How well does my child handle the transition from one activity to another? Some children find it difficult to switch gears. This is an opportunity for you to share with the teacher how you handle the situation at home. Are there any tips that you've found make it easier? For example, how do you handle the tricky period when it's time to end playtime and get ready for bed?

4. Are there any children she especially enjoys and might like to have a play date with after school?

5. How are her fine-motor skills developing (coloring, using scissors, building with small cubes); how are her large-motor skills developing (climbing, jumping, tumbling)?

The fall conference is also an opportunity to discuss what you are hearing from your child about school. Here is your chance to bring up any concerns you may have, either about school or about child development in general. Your child's teacher can be a strong and reassuring resource. Come prepared. You expect the teacher to organize herself for the conference. You should too.

The Spring Conference

Now your child has been in school for six or more months. The teacher has had an opportunity to observe and get to know both your youngster—and you. This is a time to discuss progress and development over the year.

1. What is happening socially? Is she branching out to new friends or close with any one particular child? How does she interact with other adults? How does she handle conflict? Sharing?

2. How are her large-motor skills developing? Is she comfortable on the playground? Does she climb the jungle gym easily? Is she able to pedal a tricycle? Bounce a ball? Catch a ball?

3. How are her fine-motor skills? Can she hold a pencil/crayon/marker comfortably? Is she able to use scissors? Can she manipulate puzzle pieces? Pour juice into a cup from a small pitcher?

For those students continuing in preschool, the spring conference is also a time to discuss placement for next year's classes. Introduce the topic if the teacher does not. You may have some suggestions for children you would like to see in your child's class. Explain your rationale for requesting a specific placement. You may think it will make the transition to the next class easier because of a close friendship between the children. Carpooling or baby-sitting requirements are also reasonable issues to bring up.

Tread tactfully on the issue of children you would prefer to see separated from your child. This is a touchy subject, but you must be honest if you believe that your child would benefit from being separated from a specific youngster.

Be sure and ask if the teacher has any specific placement ideas. For example, the teacher may suggest separating two friends if she feels that one or both are limiting their social opportunities because they interact solely with each other. If you disagree, be honest and open about your reasoning. You may be able to add a perspective that the teacher doesn't have. For example, your child may only see this friend at school and interacts well with others outside of school. Or you may believe that your child needs the security of a special friend in class, especially if there are stressful situations, such as a new sibling, at home.

While this is an equally touchy subject, you may find it important to discuss placement with a specific teacher. Many schools don't give parents an option, but if you have a specific reason why you think your child will benefit from being with a certain teacher, say so. Generally, it's more productive to say why you think your child *should be with* someone, rather than why *he should not* be with a particular individual. For example, you might point out that your child is especially interested in science and you've noticed that a certain teacher shares this enthusiasm. Ask the teacher if it's necessary to discuss these placement issues with the school director.

If your child will be entering kindergarten in the fall, you'll also want to discuss any reading readiness your child may be showing. (See Chapter 8 for general discussion of kindergarten readiness.) Ask the teacher if there is any information she feels you should share with the kindergarten teacher.

Body Language and Presentation Speaks Volumes

Sometimes it's not the message, but the way that it is delivered that is the problem. One experienced preschool teacher confided that she, too, was nervous when she attended her own children's conferences. She always asked her husband: "So what did you think of the *tone* of the conversation?" Even if all the right words were said, were they believable? Was there any undercurrent or hidden meaning? Parents worry—it's a fact of life!

Choose your words carefully when presenting what appears to be a criticism of the teacher or the school. *Don't hesitate to bring up an uncomfortable topic. You owe it to your child to be honest about the situation—but avoid words that will inflame a situation.* It's quite possible that the teacher is unaware that the child is troubled; or there may be a specific reason why the teacher has chosen a certain approach with your son or daughter (even if you think it is wrong).

Body language can also affect open communication.

✎ Make eye contact to show interest and concern.
✎ Crossing your arms or legs may indicate a defensive position or anger.
✎ Lean toward the speaker to indicate attentiveness.

Arrive on Time and Leave Promptly

Respect the conference schedule. If you will be late or have to reschedule, call ahead. This shows the teachers that you consider their time as valuable as your own. Since several conferences may be scheduled for the morning, one following another, if you feel you need additional time or that there are topics that still need to be discussed, don't hesitate to make another appointment.

What to Say When You Come Home

Be sure and take the time to tell your preschooler some of the *positive* highlights of the conference. She'll want to know what you saw in her classroom (mention if you saw a painting or building that she made), as well as the many complimentary comments the teacher made about her. It will make your child feel good about school and her teacher, as well as establish in your child's mind the partnership between school and home.

Conferences should be a learning experience for parents and the teacher. All parties should emerge from a meeting with a better understanding of their main concern, your child.

If There Is a Problem

Crises should be discussed and handled as they happen, but the conference is a time for parents and teacher to share approaches in handling everyday child-care issues. For example, a teacher was concerned that a little girl couldn't seem to stop chattering during story time and had tried "time-outs" as a way of controlling the problem. But the parents were able to point out that the family had recently moved to the area and perhaps the child was anxious to make new friends. The teacher was delighted to put the situation in perspective and altered her approach to the problem.

What should come out of any discussion is a common approach to the resolution of the problem. If your child is having difficulty sharing, or cleaning up, or hitting, etc., you want to be sure that the issue is thoroughly discussed and that you are presenting a united front in dealing with your child. Nothing is more confusing to a youngster than to get one message at school, and a different one at home.

Pinpointing the Problem

Declaring "I hate school" or insisting that "I don't want to go to school," are obvious signs that there is a problem, but the symptoms that your child is troubled about school may be more subtle. You may see more clinginess when it's time to leave him at school; there may be a change in behavior either at school or at home—more tantrums, contrariness; he may be having new or different problems relating to other youngsters; he may have difficulty sleeping or regress in toileting. Your child may not be able to articulate exactly what is the problem at school, so you will have to play detective.

Start by talking to your child. Perhaps he can explain what is bothering him. You may need to take an indirect route if your child can't or won't talk. Sometimes a youngster opens up when he expresses his feelings *through* puppets. One little girl, who had initially enjoyed school, but had recently balked at going, confided in a puppet that she didn't like it when her teacher had yelled at her. This gave the mother the information she needed to ask the teacher about the incident and, together, develop a plan to ease the child's fears.

Next, talk to the teacher. She may already be aware that there is a problem. Working together to determine what is bothering your child—and then joining forces to find a solution—is most helpful for your youngster. If the teacher is not aware that there is a problem, then she needs to hear what you are seeing at home.

Here are some other techniques to help pinpoint a problem if your child can't articulate what it is that is bothering her.

✎ Talk to classmates' parents to see if other children are being similarly affected.

✎ Spend some time in the classroom. The problem may lie with someone other than the teacher. Perhaps your child is having problems with transitions, frustrated over a piece of equipment—or even something as simple as not liking the juice at snack and being afraid to say so.

✎ Ask the school director to observe the class over several days. Ask for a joint conference with the teacher to problem solve. If it is a question of teacher-child incompatibility, you will need the school director to resolve the problem. (See following section for suggestions.)

Suppose You Disagree

Picking your battles is important in raising children—and for that matter, getting along in this world. Your child's teacher may have a different method of handling problems than you do—and that's okay if it's not an issue you consider vital. For example, it may be the policy of the school to say a prayer before snack or a meal. This may not be your custom at home, but presumably you wouldn't have chosen this school if this practice offended you.

On the other hand, one preschool teacher discussed, with some concern, a three-year-old's frequent "tuning out" during class and not paying attention to directions. The mother didn't see a behavior problem, but rather, knowing the youngster's problems with ear infections, immediately took her son for a medical checkup. It turns out that the little boy had an accumulation of fluid in his ears that was seriously affecting his hearing. He wasn't "tuning out," he just couldn't hear.

The point is that you have to rely on your own instincts, even if you are a first-time parent. While you want to be a good listener, if something doesn't ring true about your child, say so.

When to Ask for Help

Hopefully, you and the teacher will be on the same wavelength about your child. But if it's a serious disagreement, you may need to have a third person arbitrate. Don't hesitate to ask the school director to be part of the discussion—and if necessary, part of the solution.

If you and the teacher cannot resolve a serious issue, you may want to ask to have your child assigned to another class. This is, of course, a last resort. It's not easy for the school, but even more important, it's not easy for your child to readjust to a new class, new friends, new teachers, and new routines. Alternatively, you can pull your child out of the school, but this is an even more extreme decision.

Remember: When you talk about the decision with your child:

1. **Try to work within the system if possible.**
2. **Ask yourself: Is this something that directly impacts on my child, or is it an issue that bothers me but has little effect on my youngster?**
3. **Are the potential benefits significantly greater than the potential costs?**

4.   Make it clear to your child that this is a "Mommy and Daddy" decision, that it is not his responsibility to make this choice, and that he is not to blame for the change.

Follow-Up Is Critical

If an important issue is raised during the conference, discuss when and how you and the teacher are going to talk again. When there has been a significant change in your child's life—a new baby at home, a divorce, a new baby-sitter—tell the school and ask that the teacher call you with a report on how, if at all, the changes are impacting on your child's classroom behavior. If there is a problem, agree to talk again in a week to see if progress is being made—and then again, if necessary.

Is It Something More Serious?

Child abuse is a scary subject and every parent's nightmare. It's important to remember, however, that sexual abuse in preschools is rare. Far more abuse happens in a child's own home at the hands of friends or relatives. That said, what are the danger signs that something seriously wrong is happening at school?

✎ **Your child show persistent signs of distress:** nightmares, unexplained crying, loss of appetite, changes in sleeping, reluctance to go to school, unexplained bruises or cuts. The problem with all of these signs is that they are not necessarily symptoms of abuse. But they are evidence that something is wrong—and you need to find out what.

✎ **Your child is overly concerned with her genitals.** Bathroom humor is typical of preschoolers, but if your youngster seems to be very protective of her private parts, or has nightmares about them, you will want to find out what's prompting the concern.

✎ **Your child doesn't want to be hugged or kissed.** Again, your youngster may be going through a phase where kissing is "yucky," but if your normally affectionate child suddenly withdraws, it may be a sign that something is wrong.

If You Suspect Abuse

If you suspect, but don't know if abuse has occurred:

1. Take your child out of the program until the question is resolved.
2. Talk to other parents. Child abuse rarely happens to just one child.
3. Visit the preschool and talk frankly to the director. Explain your suspicions and ask for an immediate investigation.

If There Is Abuse

1. **Take your child out of school if you have not already done so.**
2. Take your child for a medical examination. Your pediatrician can help you and your child deal with this horrible experience. Your doctor can recommend a therapist if you feel that your child—and you—need help dealing with this crisis.
3. Report the crime (and it is a crime). Go to the police. You may also want to contact the district attorney and the child welfare board.
4. Contact the other parents in the school.

Most of all, let your child know by telling him or her over and over again:

1. It is not his/her fault in any way, shape, or form.
2. While some adults may do bad things, most grown-ups do not hurt children.
3. You will always love him/her and believe him/her.
4. He/she can tell you anything and it won't change how much you love him/her.
5. It is your job to take care of him/her and protect him/her.

While this is a terrifying, horrendous experience for your family, the love and support you give your child during a crisis will make a difference in terms of long-term recovery.

Questions and Answers

Q: My husband and I have recently separated. How should we handle school conferences? Should we attend together or ask for separate meetings?

A: There's no question that even with the best intentions, separation and divorce will have an enormous impact on your child. There's no getting around it, and parents should be prepared to deal with their youngster's reactions, which may include regression, anger, fear. Don't assume that the kids are too young to notice, or that even if you and your partner have been arguing frequently, that the children will prefer the peace and quiet.

With few exceptions, children show or act out some of their concerns in school. Your child may be confused or frightened by all the changes in her life. If you are sharing custody, she may be anxious on days when she switches caregivers. The teachers need to have information about your separation, as well as custody arrangements. This isn't prying, but vital knowledge that will help the teacher help your child.

Some couples are able to put aside differences and attend conferences together. But this is effective *only* if both partners can discuss issues without rancor and anger with each other. Your child may be exhibiting immature or hostile behavior in school in reaction to your separation, so it's important, if difficult, to listen carefully to what the teacher is observing. Again, the school should not be sitting in judgment, even if the preschool school is affiliated with a religious institution that prohibits divorce. You need an impartial, sympathetic perspective on your youngster.

Don't use the conference to assign blame for any problems that your child is experiencing. If, on the other hand, the parents cannot attend the conference amicably, it's reasonable to request separate, *confidential* meetings. Again, it's important to use the conference to understand your child and what is happening at school. Do not ask the teacher to serve as a conduit between parents (that's what lawyers are for), nor ask for information about the other partner.

Q: I walked out of my son's conference worried about an off-handed comment that the teacher had made. She said that my son tended to go off into his own world, and when I asked if this could be a problem in the future, she answered that "if they're teaching how to read on a day he decides to tune out, he may not learn." Should I have him privately tested?

A: Before making an appointment for testing, ask the teacher for another meeting, either by telephone or in person. Explain your concerns and question just how serious the problem may be. The teacher may have been joking since learning to read is not a single-day process. The teacher may have meant that your son has strong powers of concentration and is able to ignore outside distractions. Ask the teacher to put your son's behavior into perspective. Is he tuning out constantly? Are there certain situations where he seems to detach himself from the group or task at hand? Is he doing this more than most children?

Ask your child if something in the classroom is upsetting him. He may be tuning out as his means of coping with a difficult situation.

While it may take a good teacher to keep your son focused when he gets into elementary school, he will learn to read. Don't permit a single comment to unduly influence you. Ask the teacher to explain herself, and you might point out, nicely, how worried you were by her comment. She may need to temper her remarks when in parent-teacher conferences.

Q: The preschool teacher complained that our daughter has difficulty moving from one activity to another, frequently gets upset, and sometimes throws a tantrum, when it's cleanup time. The teacher asked us what we do at home

153

with this behavior and frankly we're stumped. We don't like it either, but time-outs don't seem to work.

A: Many children have trouble with transition, leaving behind a fun activity and moving on to another project, even when the new activity is fun too. It's often helpful to give fair warning about a change. Suggest to the teacher that she try to give five-minutes notice before cleanup time, alerting your daughter that she will soon have to leave what she is doing. Ask the teacher to compliment your daughter when she handles a transition well. Try this same technique at home. This is a situation where it helps if both home and school work together.

Q: I walked out of my daughter's conference absolutely furious. I felt like the teacher had absolutely no clue about my child. And yet, my daughter seems to like the teacher and has made friends. Should I take her out of the program?

A: Under the circumstances, you would be wise to ask for a conference with the school director. Explain, without anger, what happened at the conference and your concerns about continuing in the school. Ask the director to observe your daughter's class and the interaction between your child and the teacher in question. The year may be salvageable, and you will avoid the disruption of changing schools, if you are right and despite your own dislike of the teacher, the classroom situation is acceptable. If you choose to keep your child in the school, ask the director to be present at any future conferences.

7

HOW THEY GROW

The Physical, Intellectual, and Emotional Changes at Ages Two, Three, Four, and Five

The preschool years are a time of tremendous physical, emotional, and intellectual growth. At each stage you want a program that will meet your child's new needs and abilities. Although each youngster develops at her own pace, the typical four-year-old is ready for different challenges than the three-year-old student, just as the three-year-old can handle more than a child a year younger. The preschool classroom and curriculum should connect with your child's changing abilities.

This period of intellectual and emotional growth is also a time of significant physical change and development. Your child will grow taller, add several pounds, and refine his large and small-motor control. Again, the curriculum and equipment should reflect these new physical capabilities.

But, of course, the curriculum can't matter much if your child is home sick rather than in school. And during the preschool years, your child, unfortunately, will probably contract one virus after another. Let's examine why—and what you can do about it.

Keeping Healthy in Preschool

Your child's immune system is developing from constant exposure to a variety of common viruses and bacteria. It's not a question of good hygiene, either at home or at school. Young children are more vulnerable than adults since immunity to certain viruses increases with age. It might sometimes seem that your youngster is out of school more than she is in.

Preschoolers seem to catch one cold after another. Ear infections for this age group are common, as is strep throat. In fact, over the course of the school year, the preschool classroom will, in fact, be a breeding ground for common childhood ailments like pink eye, stomach virus, flu, and head lice.

And, of course, the big questions about preschool illness are: Does my child have to stay home—and for how long? One mother, calculating the per diem cost of nursery school, figured out that each sick day cost her $30. "I understood the school rules about keeping my child home when she is sick, but it seemed my daughter caught a cold in September that lasted until May. If she had stayed home with everyday sniffles, she would probably have been in school for less than a week over the course of the school year."

Why Are Preschoolers So Vulnerable?

Why are young children at risk? Let's take the common cold as an example. It may seem like one continuous sniffle, but there are actually more than 200 rhinoviruses that cause similar coldlike symptoms. Your child will develop antibodies on a virus-by-virus

BETTER NOW, THAN LATER

It's better for your child to get most of these common childhood illnesses as a youngster than as an adult. In general, the common childhood illnesses are fairly mild when contracted by a young child, but they can be more painful and result in more serious complications if an adult develops the disease.

basis—which accounts for many colds. The ear infections that often accompany a cold, the result of fluid build up in the middle ear, occur because preschooler ears often don't drain efficiently (a self-correcting condition as they grow older).

The preschool classroom, enclosed and sometimes overheated, is a perfect breeding ground for viruses, which flourish in warm, dry places. The chances of transmission are higher because the germs can't escape the environment. And in these close quarters, young children are often clustered together around the snack table or on a mat during circle time. They are constantly being exposed whenever a child sneezes or coughs. And chances are that with 15 children in the class someone is always coming down with something!

Viruses are also transmitted whenever one preschooler touches an infected child (or discarded tissue), then touches his own nose or mouth. Further, a cold virus can live for several hours on countertops and toys.

Is it any wonder that preschoolers seem to have constant runny noses?

In Sickness and in Health

In this section we'll describe the most common preschool illnesses, the length of contagion, and how long the child has to remain at home. **This section is intended to give parents a general idea of illnesses that frequently affect preschoolers. The symptoms can apply to other ailments.**

It is always wise to consult your pediatrician. Parents are advised to speak with their doctor before administering any medication.

When to keep your child home? The general rules of common sense apply.

1. **Fever**   If your child has a fever, keep her at home until her temperature has been normal for 24 hours.
2. **Antibiotics**   If your child needs antibiotics, keep her at home until she has been on the medication at least 24 hours.

AN OUNCE OF PREVENTION

No matter what you do, no matter how careful and clean your home and your child's school are, your child will be exposed to a variety of bacteria and viruses as she grows. So is there anything you can do to reduce the number of common colds and childhood ailments she contracts? Here are some basic cold/disease busters:

1. **Wash hands**   This is the number one best piece of advice for reducing disease. Soap and water kill germs. Teach your children to wash after going to the bathroom, playing in the dirt, and before eating. Model that behavior for them. Insist on this practice at preschool.
2. **Follow good diaper-changing hygiene**   The changing table cover should be cleaned and disinfected after every diaper change, whether or not disposable paper is used. Disposable paper should be discarded after each diaper change. The diaper pail should be covered.
3. **Avoid closed, heated rooms**   Cold viruses flourish in warm, dry places, and the chances of transmission are higher because the germs can't escape the environment. Fresh air can help reduce the transmission of infection. Ventilate your house thoroughly at least once a day either by opening a window or through an internal ventilation system. Make sure this is common practice at the preschool.
4. **Sanitize toys and surfaces**   Because young children tend to put toys in their mouths, it's important to clean and disinfect toys and surfaces on a daily basis.
5. **Stay away from people with obvious colds**   This isn't easy when a child is in preschool. Insist that the school has a clear policy on how long a child must stay out of school for most common problems and what conditions must be met before a child can return to school.
6. **Teach your child to cover his nose and mouth when he sneezes or coughs.**   After coughing or sneezing, he should wash his hands with soap and water.
7. **Dispose of tissues properly after each use.**   Do not save or reuse.

> **WARNING: NEVER GIVE ASPIRIN TO A YOUNG CHILD.**
>
> The combination of aspirin and viral infection is associated with Reye's syndrome, a potentially fatal disease of the liver and brain.

3. **Pink or running eyes** If your child's eyes are pink or she has mucus running out of one or both eyes, keep her at home until you receive a definite diagnosis from your doctor.
4. **Undiagnosed rash** Keep your child home until either the rash clears up or there is a firm diagnosis on what it is and whether it is contagious.
5. **Diarrhea/vomiting** Keep your child home until the diarrhea or vomiting has stopped.
6. **Head lice** Keep your child at home until she has received appropriate treatment and all nits have been removed.

Common Cold

A viral infection of the upper respiratory tract. Even very healthy children catch about six colds a year. Colds are caused by exposure to viruses, not by being out in the cold or getting wet.

Symptoms Stuffy or runny nose, sneezing, headache, sore throat, cough, loss of appetite, watery or burning eyes, ear congestion, low-grade fever, aching muscles and joints

Duration Five to seven days, barring complications

Contagious? Yes. Symptoms appear within one or two days of exposure.

Treatment No antibiotics. Over-the-counter medications to relieve symptoms. Acetaminophen or ibuprofen to relieve fever and ease aching bones and joints. Decongestants decrease swelling and inflammation in nasal cavity, providing relief from stuffy or runny nose; cough syrup relieves constant cough. Use a cool-mist humidifier in child's room. Have youngster drink plenty of fluids to thin secretions, which makes it easier for the body to clear them.

Stay Home?   **No**, as long as there is no fever, no signs of more serious illness, and child feels well enough to participate in school activities.

Danger Signs: **Call your doctor if your child's temperature spikes and remains high for 72 hours, his throat becomes extremely sore, if he has difficulty breathing or complains of an earache.**

Ear Infection

Bacterial infection of fluid buildup in middle ear, a frequent complication of a cold.

Symptoms   Pain in the ear, child may have fever. May have feeling of fullness or pressure in the ear. May experience a temporary slight hearing loss.

Contagious?   No

Duration   Fluid may last for one week or more, even after symptoms have disappeared. Patient must complete course of antibiotics treatment and be checked by doctor to be certain that the infection is completely gone.

Treatment   Antibiotics and may prescribe decongestant.

Stay Home?   **Yes**, generally one day if accompanied by fever and pain. Child ran return to school after a 24-hour dose of antibiotics if she feels well enough to participate in activities.

Cough

Coughing is the body's method of expelling excess mucus from the lungs. It is a common complication after a cold. Cough may linger or even intensify after the cold symptoms have begun to dissipate. Unfortunately, too much coughing can irritate the lung passages and lead to more coughing.

Symptoms   If accompanied by fever, fatigue, difficulty in breathing may be symptomatic of more serious infection. Check with your doctor.

Contagious?   Yes, can spread virus through expelled mucus.

Duration   Can last several weeks after cold symptoms have dissipated.

Treatment   If cough is complication of a cold, doctor may recommend over-the-counter cough suppressant with dextromethorphan (marked on label with DM) or in more severe cases doctor may prescribe cough suppressant with codeine. Check with your doctor if the cough is keeping your child up at night or if it lasts more than two weeks.

Stay home? **No,** unless child does not feel well enough to participate in activities.

Strep Throat

Streptococcal infection is easily treated with antibiotics, but can lead to serious complications if left untreated. Doctor confirms diagnosis with a throat culture. Results available within 24 hours (some tests give results within 15 minutes).

Symptoms Sore throat, fever, headache, swollen glands

Contagious? Yes, within two to three days of exposure

Duration Symptoms dissipate within 48 hours of treatment, but patient must complete course of antibiotics to avoid possibility of serious complications.

Treatment Antibiotics

Stay Home? **Yes,** child can return to school after 24-hour dose of antibiotics.

Scarlet Fever

Streptococcal infection, which may develop 12 hours to two days after strep throat symptoms appear. Doctor will confirm diagnosis with a throat culture.

Symptoms Similar to symptoms for strep throat, fever, headache, sore throat, may vomit. Child may be sick for a day before rash comes out. Rash resembles a red blush and begins in warm, moist parts of body (armpits, groin, back). May also have red, swollen, "strawberry tongue."

Contagious? Yes, within two to three days of exposure

Duration Rash lasts about seven days after which skin begins to peel or flake off.

Treatment Antibiotics

Stay Home? **Yes,** if child feels better, can return to school after rash disappears and 24 hours on medication.

Influenza (the Flu)

Viral infection of the respiratory tract.

Symptoms Chills, fever, headache, aches and pains, fatigue, lack of appetite

Contagious? Yes, two days before symptoms appear and until the fifth day of illness

Duration Three to five days

Treatment Antibiotics ineffective. Treatment directed at relieving symptoms such as acetaminophen or ibuprofen for fever and aches.

Stay home? **Yes**, for duration of illness.

Conjunctivitis

Inflammation of the white of the eye, can be bacterial, viral, or an allergic reaction

Symptoms Eye redness, puslike discharge, pain

Contagious? Yes, within two or three days of exposure

Duration Lasts five to seven days

Treatment Warm water compresses, applied for 10 minutes, four to six times per day. If using a cotton ball, discard after use. If using cloth, wash, *separately*, in hot water and detergent before using again. After examination, the doctor may prescribe antibiotics in form of eye drops or ointment, if diagnosed as bacterial infection.

Stay Home? **Yes**, if bacterial. Child can return to school after 24-hour dose of antibiotics.

Impetigo

Skin infection caused by either streptococcus or staphylococcus bacteria, which if left untreated can cause serious complications.

Symptoms Brownish yellow (honey-colored) scabs or crusts. Begins with pimple with yellowish/white blister, which gets rubbed off and scab forms. Often begins on face, but spreads when hand touches scab and then touches other body parts.

Contagious? Yes, within one or two days of exposure

Duration Lasts seven to 10 days

Treatment Antibiotics

Stay Home? Yes, child can return to school after 24-hour dose of antibiotics.

Danger Signs: **Call your doctor if there is an increase in the number or size of the sores, if your child develops a fever, sore throat, blood in the urine, or swollen eyelids.**

Ringworm

Fungal infection of the outer layers of the scalp, skin, and nails. It is not actually a worm. It is the same fungus that causes "jock itch" and "athlete's foot."

Symptoms Circular patch of rough skin, raised edge, clear center, about the size of a nickel. Outer rim is composed of little bumps. If in the scalp, round patches of skin with hair broken off short. Appearance of dandruff in young child is suspicious.

Contagious? Yes, from contaminated surfaces such as shower stalls in a gym or gymnasium floors. Can also be contracted from an infected animal.

Duration Can be persistent, can last several weeks. If left untreated can lead to chronic rash or hair loss.

Treatment Topical antifungals applied for a full course of treatment (up to three weeks, although symptoms generally improve within one week). If in the scalp, use a shampoo that contains selenium sulfide for at least one week.

Stay Home? **Yes**, child can return to school after 24 hours of medication.

Fifth Disease

Erythema infectiosum is an infectious viral disease, sometimes called "the slapped cheek disease." It got the name "fifth disease" years ago when it was listed fifth on a register of the (then) most common causes of rash and fever in childhood: measles, mumps, chicken pox, and rubella. While it causes only mild symptoms in children, researchers are studying whether it causes birth defects in the babies of pregnant women who contract the disease. Outbreaks commonly begin in late winter and spring.

Symptoms Mild flulike symptoms the first week with low-grade fever, sore throat, and runny nose. The child then develops a rash on the face, which resembles a "slapped cheek," and appears lacy looking on the arms and legs. The rash doesn't itch.

Contagious? Only *before* the rash appears

Duration The rash usually fades over two to three weeks, but may recur for up to three months, especially after a hot bath or vigorous physical activity.

Treatment None, except acetaminophen to relieve fever, if necessary.

Stay home? **No,** since period of contagion is over once the rash appears, unless the child has fever or feels unable to participate in activities.

Stomachache, Vomiting, Diarrhea

Symptoms of a variety of illnesses, from the common cold to more serious ailments such as intestinal flu or appendicitis. May be caused by virus, bacteria, or as the result of mild food poisoning.

Symptoms Check with your doctor if your child has a stomachache that lasts more than an hour, whether it is severe or not. If diarrhea lasts more than 48 hours, contact your doctor. If vomiting accompanies diarrhea and persists for more than 24 hours, check with your doctor. Check with your doctor if fever accompanies gastrointestinal upsets, or if the conditions increase in intensity or frequency. Dehydration is a concern when a child has persistent diarrhea or vomiting.

Contagious? Yes, if caused by virus, bacteria, or protozoa. No, if gastrointestinal upset due to food poisoning.

Duration If intestinal flu, lasts one to three days.

Treatment For a stomachache: do not give any medication without checking with doctor.

For vomiting: no medication without checking with doctor. Keep up fluids.

For diarrhea: For mild cases, give bananas, avoid milk products, supplement fluids. Check with your doctor before giving any over-the-counter medication.

Stay Home? **Yes,** until symptoms disappear.

Danger Signs: **Call your doctor if your child is urinating infrequently, has a parched, dry mouth, cries without tears, or has**

sunken eyes. These are signs of dehydration. Also check with your doctor if your child has prolonged or severe abdominal pain.

Lyme Disease

Illness caused by a spirochete (a slender, spiral-shaped bacterium) spread by infected deer ticks. The ticks are so small (about the size of the period at the end of a sentence) that they are easily overlooked when on the body. Often ignored in the early stages because it mimics other ailments (like flu), it can lead to long-term, neurological damage if left untreated. Originally identified in Lyme, Connecticut, but now found in most areas of the United States. A blood test confirms the disease, but if negative and symptoms persist, the test may have to be repeated as it is usually not positive for several weeks after infection is contracted.

Symptoms   Characteristic "bull's eye" marking at the site of the tick bite (generally, but not always on arm or leg). It is a round, raised reddish lesion with a paler center. Your child may also have flulike symptoms such as fever, chills, headache, overall achiness, fatigue, malaise.

Contagious?   No, not from person to person, only from tick bite. Symptoms Can develop from three days to three weeks or more from initial tick bite.

Duration   Symptomatic relief generally after completing course of antibiotic treatment of 10 to 20 days, but fatigue and achiness often last for weeks.

Treatment   Antibiotics given orally for 10 to 20 days. Intravenous antibiotics may be prescribed if disease is more advanced.

Stay home?   No, if child feels well enough to participate in activities.

Chicken Pox

Disease caused by the varicella-zoster virus, a member of the herpes family. A vaccine is available and recommended by the American Academy of Pediatrics (AAP). It is administered when the child is between 12 and 18 months, with a second dose administered between the ages of 11 and 12. Immunization is not uniformly required by school districts for entry into kindergarten. Check with your preschool for their policy on the chicken pox vaccine. Although the AAP recommends the vaccine, some parents have opted not to have their child immunized. Chicken pox is still a problem in many preschools.

Chicken pox is a relatively mild disease (although it can be extremely uncomfortable for the patient), but the potential complications, although rare, can be very serious, even fatal.

Symptoms   One to two days before blisters appear, child may have moderate fever, headache, fatigue, sore throat, achiness. Rash begins as flat and reddish, generally on the trunk of the body and one or two days later spreads to extremities, neck, and face. Turns from red rash to masses of tiny, itchy pimples and then into blisters.

Contagious?   A child is contagious for one or two days before any symptoms appear. Once blisters erupt, a child continues to be contagious until all of the blisters are dry and have formed scabs (four or five days). A child develops symptoms of the disease between 11 and 21 days after exposure.

Duration   Lasts about two weeks

Treatment   Over-the-counter medication, such as calamine lotion, helps to relieve itching and dry weeping sores. Oatmeal baths are very soothing. Acetaminophen may be used to bring down fever and relieve pain.

Stay home?   **Yes,** until all blisters are dry and have formed scabs.

Danger Signs: **Call your doctor if your child has difficulty waking up, trouble walking, a stiff neck, difficulty breathing, repeated vomiting, high fever.**

Let's Talk about Head Lice

Yuk! is the almost universal response when you bring up the topic of head lice. But this nasty little problem has been around since ancient Egypt. Six million children are affected each year. Although they can be a problem any time of the year, September brings peak incidence.

Head lice are a pain to deal with, but **absolutely no reflection on your family's hygiene.** In fact, head lice prefer clean hair and scalps to dirty ones. Regular shampoo and water are ineffective against head lice. Because they spread easily, eliminating lice requires careful, step-by-step treatment, follow-up checks, and often a coordinated school-wide effort. **Much as you might prefer never to speak of head lice, you will need to be honest—and insist on honesty from your child's classmates and play dates—when it comes to head lice. You need to know if your child has been exposed.**

What Are Head Lice?

Pediculosis, the medical term for head lice infestation, is caused by tiny parasitic insects that attach themselves to the scalp. It's a question of proximity. The insects are spread through direct contact. For example, lice are easily transmitted when: an infected child sits next to another youngster at the snack table; the knit hat of an infected child lays on top of his classmate's hat; the stuffed animal of an infected child is passed around the classroom. In the family, if one child is infected everyone should be checked for lice.

Head lice are small, about the size of a sesame seed. They live by biting and sucking blood from the scalp. They cannot survive for more than a few hours unless they are on a human head. Head lice itch and the constant scratching can lead to secondary infections.

It can be one to three weeks after infestation for itching to begin, but by then, there may be a large number of lice in your child's hair. A single louse can lay between 90 and 100 eggs!

Symptoms

The most obvious symptom is that your child complains of an itchy head or you notice him scratching persistently. The lice prefer the area behind the ears and the nape of the neck, but can be found anywhere on the head.

Check your child's scalp. Head lice are about 1/16 inch long, gray/brown, and move very quickly. You may not be able to see any. The nits, the egg cases, are easier to spot. They resemble little specks that look like tiny white rice grains or dandruff stuck on a hair shaft. The giveaway is that they do not come off the hair shaft easily when flicked.

A Step-by-Step Treatment Program

Eradicating lice is basically a three-step process: killing the adult lice, removing the nits, and cleaning the home (school) environment.

1. **Medicated shampoo**   Use an over-the-counter lice/nit killing shampoo. Follow directions carefully. A prescription shampoo, such as Lindane, is effective, but may be toxic to the nervous system. Check with your doctor if conventional treatment is not working and a more toxic shampoo is necessary. **Do not use multiple applications of any medicated shampoo without first checking with your doctor.**

2. **Comb out the nits**   This is the tedious, but *absolutely essential* step necessary to rid your child of lice. If even one nit is left, it can cause a reinfestation. With a good light overhead, separate the hair into one-inch sections. Using a fine-toothed comb, and taking it virtually hair by hair, remove all nits. You can also remove the nits by grasping them between your thumb and forefinger and pulling them down and off the hair shaft.

    Parent tip: This is a perfect time for a video. One family, in the midst of a school-wide lice epidemic, was infected three times. The mother would pop in a one-hour cartoon video and, as the child watched, methodically comb out her daughter's hair. If a nit is stuck and won't come off easily, cut off the hair shaft it's on.

3. **Lice-busting home cleanup**   Because lice need a human host to live, if you rid your house of nits that have migrated onto the blankets, the stuffed animals, the rugs, you will lessen your chance of reinfestation. Here's the exhausting, but necessary steps to take.

✎ Wash all clothes, bedding, combs and brushes in **hot** water—sheets, blankets, comforters, towels, hats, scarves—dry at least 20 minutes in hot cycle in dryer.

✎ Dry-clean that which cannot be washed—coats, woolens.

✎ Vacuum pillows, rugs, furniture, *and the car* and discard bag.

✎ Suffocate that which can't be washed, vacuumed, or dry cleaned: put stuffed animals in a plastic garbage bag, seal the bag, and leave it for **two weeks.**

✎ Discard or disinfect combs and brushes by soaking them in hot water (130 to 150 degrees Fahrenheit) or hot water and medicated shampoo for 20 minutes.

Parent tip: Freeze stuffed animals to rid them of nits. Put the stuffed toys, overnight or longer, in a freezing environment (below 30 degrees).

Preventive Measures

1. Check your child every night for nits, whether she is itching or not. Recheck for several weeks. If you find any nits, consider only those that are near the scalp as evidence of reinfestation. You will probably find missed nits, which become more apparent as the hair grows. **Do not treat again with medicated shampoo unless you are certain your child has been reinfested.**

2. Check everyone in the family. Lice spread like wildfire in a family.

3. Teach your child not to share things that go on or near the head (for example, never use someone else's comb or hat).

4. Keep long hair in tight braids so that the lice will have less hair to which they can attach.

A MESSY BUT EFFECTIVE HOME REMEDY

If you are concerned about the chemicals in the lice-killing shampoos, there is an old-fashioned technique that is nontoxic and successful. Rub your child's hair and scalp with petroleum jelly, soft margarine (about one large tub) or vegetable shortening. Make a plastic wrap turban to cover the hair and leave it on for several hours. You'll want to watch your child carefully during that time so that she doesn't play with the plastic wrap and put it over her mouth or nose. Don't allow your child to sleep while wearing it. This method suffocates the lice. Shampoo with a nonmedicated product and remove all nits as described above.

MORE PARENT-TESTED PREVENTION TIPS

✎ As a preventative measure, use rosemary shampoo or apply a little rosemary oil or lotion behind the ears.

✎ Another possible repellant is tea-tree oil. Massage into the scalp and wrap the head in a warm towel to help it penetrate.

5. Vacuum rugs, furniture, bedding, coats, and stuffed animals regularly.
6. Until you are sure that your child is lice free, wash her clothes, sheets, towels separately in hot water.

If There Is a Lice Epidemic at Preschool

1. Insist that each child's coat, hat, and backpack are kept in a sealed plastic garbage bag during school. This keeps lice from jumping from coat to coat in crowded cubbies.
2. Do not send stuffed animals or cloth dolls to school. They are a perfect breeding ground for lice. If your child needs a transitional object from home at school, send a favorite book or plastic toy with him.
3. Ask that the school alert parents when a child in the class contracts lice. No names are necessary, but it puts a family on alert to be more vigilant about checking their child each day.

Immunizations: The Key to Good Health

Of course, you want to protect your child from 10 serious diseases—and you can. Make sure your child is immunized against diphtheria, pertussis, tetanus, polio, measles, mumps, rubella, Haemophilus influenzae type B, hepatitis B, and chicken pox, at appropriate ages (See Appendix 2 for the American Academy of Pediatrics Recommended Childhood Immunization Schedule.)

✎ Keep a record of your child's vaccinations and make sure it is up to date. Although the American Academy of Pediatrics has a suggested immunization schedule, your child may inadvertently miss a scheduled vaccine because of illness. One mother discovered, when her child was registering for college (!), that he never had his second dose of measles, mumps, and rubella vaccine.

✎ **Check with your pediatrician annually for updates on the immunization schedule.**

✎ **Insist that the preschool require that all students have up-to-date immunizations, and keep accurate medical records.**

What's Happening at Two, Three, Four, and Five

The curriculum for the twos, threes and fours at preschool, on the surface, may appear similar. All the classes are learning about their families and the natural world. But as children grow and develop, they are more capable of independent, abstract, and complex thinking. How they approach the subject, what they learn, and how they can use the information will change as they grow older. Since children progress at different rates, the classroom experience must be flexible enough to meet the needs of all the students. But the basic learning tool is the same for young children: learning by doing.

In the next sections we'll review the language, physical, intellectual, and social/emotional development of twos, threes, fours, and fives. The preschool curriculum should complement and encourage this development.

Remember: *Every child develops at her own pace. These guidelines are general. There is a broad range of what is considered "normal." It's not unusual for a child to be advanced in one area, lag slightly in another. Check with your doctor if you have any concerns.*

The Two-Year-Old

As they make the transition from baby to toddler to independent two-year-old, the going can sometimes be rough, but the results are exciting. It's understandable why this period is called the *"terrible twos,"* when tantrums and *"NO!"* are frequent occurrences. They have intense feelings and mood swings. Two-year-olds are frequently frustrated as they seek to assert their independence, but can't do more because their language and physical skills can't meet their needs and desires. For example, they want to be able to dress themselves completely, but they don't have the fine-motor control to button, zip, or buckle. They have boundless energy, but fight naps. They want to be independent, but often have difficulty separating from parents or caregiver. They have increased fearfulness of the dark, monsters, etc. Add to the mix the emotional demands of toilet training and it all adds up to a sometimes turbulent period.

But it's also the *"terrific twos"* because they are more independent, more interested in peers, and more able to concentrate on a project. They thrive on exploration and enjoy fantasy play (a piece of cloth can become a blanket for a doll or a stuffed dog may be imagined to be alive). Twos are developing a sense of humor and are increasingly able to use words to express their needs and emotions.

LANGUAGE

They are learning about:

- ✎ simple books, puzzles, pictures
- ✎ how to enjoy music and rhythm, simple fingerplay
- ✎ new words and forming complete and increasingly complex sentences (vocabulary may be around 200 words); using adjectives and adverbs ("a big red ball"; "he ran fast")
- ✎ listening to stories (may have short attention span)
- ✎ identifying objects in pictures

PHYSICAL

They are developing:

- ✎ large-motor skills. They can kick a ball, walk up and down stairs, and can put on a cap or slippers.
- ✎ fine-motor skills. They can scribble with marker (fat shaft); may be able to thread large beads; feed self with spoon; begin to pour juice from small container to small cup.

INTELLECTUAL

They are learning about:

- ✎ classification, in broad categories, such as hard/soft; large/small.
- ✎ body parts, can name nose, eyes, mouth, etc.
- ✎ short time concepts such as yesterday and tomorrow (but still have no concrete understanding of longer periods of time—months, weeks)
- ✎ how to recount the events of the morning/day.
- ✎ how to enjoy the *process* of art projects, rather than being interested in product

SOCIAL/EMOTIONAL

They are learning about:

- ✎ interactive play, but still tend to parallel play alongside a peer.
- ✎ taking turns, but often with difficulty.
- ✎ taking pride in creations and accomplishments ("I can do it!")
- ✎ feelings and frequently display aggressive behaviors and increased fearfulness

The Three-Year-Old

What a delightful age! They are becoming social animals—interested in playing with other children, beginning to share and take turns. They are learning to separate from you. Small-group activities are more effective than large-group activities. The classroom curriculum should focus on language, activity, and movement. Large-motor skills are developing quickly: threes need to ride wheel toys, climb, jump, run, kick a ball. For any activity, the process is more important than the finished product.

LANGUAGE

The are learning about:

- ✎ writing their own name (may be able to write first letter)
- ✎ pretend writing (scribble)
- ✎ sitting and listening to a book in a group

✎ speaking to a group
✎ looking at books
✎ playing rhyming games and songs
✎ new vocabulary
✎ telling a story to accompany their artwork
✎ drawing stick figures (may not have anatomical details, such as fingers)

PHYSICAL
They are developing their:

✎ large-motor skills. They can run, jump, climb, ride a tricycle, walk up stairs with one foot on each step.
✎ small-motor skills. They can use a brush, crayon, marker, (preferably with a fat shaft); string beads; build with large Legos; unzip; draw a circle.

INTELLECTUAL
They are learning about:

✎ colors, shapes
✎ things that are alike and those that are different
✎ spatial relationships: over/under; near/far
✎ the world around them: seasons, weather, animals, plants
✎ counting from 1 to 10

SOCIAL/EMOTIONAL
They are learning about:

✎ separating from home
✎ making a transition to a new setting
✎ themselves, their families, other families
✎ the classroom as a community
✎ interacting with new adults
✎ following classroom routines (e.g., snack time, cleanup)
✎ identifying body parts, feelings (happy, sad, angry), and needs ("I want to paint"; "I want more juice")
✎ self-control ("use your words, not your hands")—although they may still have problems remembering the rules)

- ✎ self-help skills (putting on coat, washing hands)
- ✎ following one-step directions ("put a napkin at each chair")
- ✎ sharing and cooperating (although don't expect them to give up favorite items or always wait patiently)

The Four-Year-Old

Four-year-olds are full of energy, enthusiasm, and curiosity. Their imaginations are working on overdrive. They are full of "whys" and can conduct a sophisticated conversation in which they incorporate the knowledge they seem to absorb. They play more cooperatively with children; enjoy fantasy and often engage in dramatic play; and are better at following rules and exercising self-control. Still, they are only four years old, and may often act impulsively. They may begin to plan ahead—"I'm going to build a parking garage with the blocks"—as opposed to building something without a plan and then finding a purpose for it. They enjoy a variety of hands-on experiences and love to learn about the workers in their community (firefighters, police officers, postal workers), and field trips enrich the preschool experience.

LANGUAGE

They are learning about:

- ✎ different kinds of books—fiction, nonfiction, poetry
- ✎ wordplay and silly songs, language
- ✎ telling a story
- ✎ using puppets to dramatize a story
- ✎ drawing pictures specifically to illustrate a story, rather than just painting or coloring
- ✎ noticing details in stories and adding details to their own stories
- ✎ predicting what will happen in a storybook using the illustrations as a guide
- ✎ singing songs and making up their own verses
- ✎ identifying letters, printing some letters, perhaps their own name, maybe others
- ✎ actively participating in a group discussion

PHYSICAL

They are developing:

- large-motor skills. They can pump a swing, climb a rope ladder, slide down a pole, skip, hop.
- fine-motor skills. They can use scissors, smaller brushes/crayons/markers, string small beads, build with smaller Legos, button.

INTELLECTUAL

They are learning about:

- sorting and classifying not only by color and size, but also by category (for example all dolls go in the bin, all the accessories go in another box)
- sequencing—can organize a series of events in order of before and after
- counting from 1 to 20 (or higher)
- cause and effect ("if I add too much juice to the cup, it will overflow"), but there is still "magical thinking" (which can be as simple as believing in Santa Claus, but also can be "if I think a bad thought, it will make it happen")
- comparison—more/less

SOCIAL/EMOTIONAL

They are learning about:

- collaborating with others on projects, cooperating, taking turns, helping others, empathy
- family roles and responsibilities
- managing fears and controlling impulses (but still have many fears and are not always in control)
- similarities and differences related to gender, race, other physical characteristics
- making choices ("I want to build with blocks, so I can't paint during free play today")
- themselves, such as their likes and preferences
- being goal directed in activities ("I want to climb to the top of the jungle gym and slide down the pole"; "I want to get all the

toy cars together and then build a garage for them out of blocks")

The Five-Year-Old

Five-year-olds are more focused and directed than younger pre-schoolers. They can cooperate in larger groups to play simple games (kickball, tag), and they plan their dramatic play with specific roles and rules for all the participants. They have rich imaginations, and their language is expressive and detailed. Friendships are very important.

LANGUAGE

They are learning about:

- ✎ all kinds of books and have personal favorites by subject or author
- ✎ recognizing all the letters of the alphabet, spelling their own name, favorite words, associating letters (consonants) with sounds
- ✎ drawing a representational picture
- ✎ retelling a story verbally, as well as through drawings or through dramatizations
- ✎ predicting what comes next in a story through pictures and story content
- ✎ participating in a class discussion, including waiting to speak until called on

PHYSICAL

They are developing:

- ✎ large-motor skills. Stronger eye-hand coordination results in improved kicking, catching, and throwing. Can play games and follow simple rules with scoring (for example, kickball).
- ✎ small-motor skills. Their grasp is more effective; can use scissors to cut on a line; manipulate tweezers or other tools (for science); and use smaller brushes, crayons, and markers.

INTELLECTUAL

They are learning about:

- sorting and classifying using two categories (for example, by size and color)
- graphing (for example, the class might develop a graph to represent family pets: how many children have dogs for pets; how many cats; how many gerbils; how many birds? Another graph might represent the students' birthdays by months: how many have birthdays in January, February, March, etc.)
- counting from 1 to 30 or higher
- writing numbers
- comparisons of greater than/less than
- calendar concepts
- estimating and measuring
- using reasoning and problem-solving skills
- basic explanations for scientific phenomena

SOCIAL/EMOTIONAL

They are learning about:

- taking responsibility for the classroom or specific chores at home (recycling, emptying the trash cans, feeding the family pet)
- conflict resolution and resolving their own problems
- better self-control and recognizing appropriate behaviors
- cooperating and compromising to keep playing with friend
- recognizing and articulating emotions and motives
- expressing empathy
- individuality and recognizing similarities and differences about self and others

Questions and Answers

Q: I work five mornings a week and thought I had the perfect child-care situation. My three-year-old daughter would be in school when I was in the office. But since school began she's had one cold, stomach virus, ear infection after another. I'm missing so many workdays I'm beginning to wonder if I would be better off not sending her to school and hiring a sitter to stay with her at home. She enjoys school when she's there, but am I doing something wrong that she's getting sick so often?

A: Stop blaming yourself. All those colds, viruses, ear infections, etc., are typical of preschoolers' health. Unless you're planning to completely isolate your child, she'd probably get many of those illnesses anyway.

What would be most helpful at this point is to figure out a good backup plan for those days when your child is sick enough that she has to stay home from school, but well enough to stay with a sitter rather than a parent. That way you could still go to work, but your child would have time to recuperate.

You'll want to hire an adult or college student as a sitter for these days. (Call your local senior center or area colleges.) Not only do older sitters bring added maturity, but they're available during school hours. You would, of course, leave complete information on how to reach you in case of emergency. If you are going to be out of the office during those hours, consider getting a cellular phone or beeper so that you are always within reach.

Another option, in certain localities, are "sick child" day-care centers. They are designed especially for kids who are mildly ill. Contact local day-care agencies to see if any of these types of "emergency drop-in" centers are in your area.

Alternatively, check to see if any family day-care homes in your area would be willing to watch your child under these circumstances (see Chapter 3 for resources).

Q: There is a lice epidemic in my son's preschool. He's been infected twice, and I'm worried about having to use all these chemicals on him. Is there anything the school can do to reduce the risk of reinfection?

A: Yes. Vigilance at home and school is required to get rid of these pesky invaders. Insist that the preschool:

1. Keep each child's coat, hat, and mittens in a closed plastic bag during school hours (to cut down on transmission of the lice).
2. Dry-clean all classroom drapes and area rugs.

3. Remove all plush animals from the classroom and put them in closed plastic bags for at least two weeks.

4. Dry-clean all dress-up clothes; remove from use any hats from the dress-up corner.

5. Most important of all, before the school day begins, have each child checked before he enters the classroom. Any infected child must be sent home immediately and may not reenter the class until treated for lice and then checked.

Q: **We were told that a child in my son's class is infected with the AIDS virus. The school director assured us that there was no risk, but I'm still worried. Suppose the infected child sneezes on my son or drinks from a cup and then shares with my child. Isn't there a risk, even if small?**

A: No case of AIDS has been transmitted in a child-care setting. The disease can't be spread by contact with urine, saliva, stool, vomit, or tears. Yes, there is some risk if your child comes in contact with infected blood, but that scenario is highly unlikely, and even then the risk is minimal.

The American Academy of Pediatrics recommends that HIV-infected children should be permitted to participate in all activities in child-care centers, since most pose no risk to others. Of course, any infected child should be under ongoing medical care, and preschool participation is premised on his current health condition. A child with a compromised immune system may be at greater risk if he contracts any common childhood ailments.

You should insist, however, that your preschool has rigorous sanitation procedures in effect and that the school staff is trained in first-aid procedures, especially when blood is present.

Q: **My almost three-year-old daughter stutters when she talks. It can be frustrating for her and for the listener to wait until she gets the whole sentence out. I'm afraid the kids in her class will make fun of her. Should she begin speech therapy?**

A: It's probably too early to suggest that your child has a speech problem. Many young children stutter and stammer. Essentially they can think faster than they can talk. Although it can be frustrating for you both, the best thing you can do to help is to allow her to finish her own sentences at her own pace. The less pressure she feels, the more comfortable she will be in talking. As her vocabulary increases and as she is better able to organize her thoughts, the stuttering will resolve itself.

The issue about teasing is separate. First, some of your concern may be transferring your own fears to what *might* happen to your child. You may be worried about something that isn't going to occur. It's quite possible that classmates may ask about your daughter's speech patterns. That's normal and not teasing. Young children frequently ask questions about anything that is different about someone—or something—else. Their insatiable curiosity leads them to blurt out whatever is on their minds.

On the other hand, if a youngster does begin to call your daughter names or make cruel remarks about your child's speech, then you should talk to the teacher. It's important that the staff set a level of tolerance that is expected from all class members, no matter how young.

8

IS MY CHILD READY
FOR KINDERGARTEN?

Preschool has been a wonderful educational experience for your child. But now, it's almost June and the days in the four-year-old class are winding down. Is your child ready for kindergarten? Or would she benefit from an extra year in preschool or perhaps a prekindergarten class, a transition program for children who are not quite ready for kindergarten?

Why Is There a Question?

Twenty-five years ago, if your child's birthday was before the cutoff date, you enrolled him in kindergarten. If the cutoff date for the district was December 31, then the ages of the kindergarten children on the first day of school might range from five years and nine months (birth date January 1) to four years and nine months (birth date December 31). And no one suggested that the younger child might be at a disadvantage developmentally or educationally.

But kindergarten was very different back then. It was much more similar to the preschool curriculum your child has just completed. The academic expectations for the students were limited. Learning to read was a first-grade subject.

Today, kindergarten, generally, is much more academically demanding. Prereading skills are emphasized, and many students will begin reading by the end of the year. While many public school systems incorporate a developmental approach to learning, many more are traditional teacher-directed programs. Desks, work sheets, larger classes, standardized testing all make for a very different environment than a preschool. A child needs to be ready to assume the challenge.

What You Need to Know about Kindergarten

Before you can make a decision about whether or not your child is ready for kindergarten, you need to familiarize yourself with your options. If you plan to send your child to a public kindergarten, make an appointment to visit the school the spring before your child will enter. This will give you an opportunity to observe and assess the program. Don't rely on hearsay from other parents to make your evaluation of the program. While it's helpful to hear opinions about kindergarten teachers, the reality is that you may not have any choice about which teacher your child is assigned, and in any case, a teacher may be a better match for your child than for someone else's.

You want to make a decision in context: Is your child ready for *this* program? Here are some questions you will want to ask:

✎ What is the prekindergarten screening procedure?
✎ When will my child be tested?
✎ Can I know the results? can I challenge them?
✎ Does the district contact the preschool for each child's records? If not, can a preschool teacher's recommendation be included in my child's permanent file?
✎ What are the class sizes? Are there any limits to the number of children in a class?
✎ Is it a full-day program?
✎ Must you attend the kindergarten in your neighborhood or can you choose to enroll in any school within the school district?

✎ Are there any magnet programs for kindergarten? (A magnet program draws children from a broad geographical area. Admission may be based on testing or some other criteria.)

✎ Do you have a choice of programs? For example, some districts might have a combined kindergarten–first grade class, as well as a straight kindergarten class. How are children chosen for each class and can you either elect or refuse an option?

Other Benchmarks

Here are some other skills that beginning kindergartners generally have. Although your child doesn't have to be proficient in all areas, the more accomplished she can be, the better.

BASIC KNOWLEDGE

Can your child say his own:

✎ name
✎ address
✎ telephone number

LANGUAGE SKILLS

Can your child express herself and be understood by adults and children?

Can your child tell a simple story?

THREE BASIC SKILLS FOR KINDERGARTEN

Rather than look at your child's age as the criterion for kindergarten enrollment, David Elkind, Ph.D., professor of child study at Tufts University, suggests that you focus on several important skills she needs for success. Is your child:

1. able to pay attention?
2. able to follow instructions?
3. able to get along with other children?

LARGE-MOTOR SKILLS

Can your child:

- climb the jungle gym
- pump on the swing
- pedal a tricycle

SMALL-MOTOR SKILLS

Can your child:

- draw a square, circle, triangle
- cut with scissors
- button and zip
- put together an eight-piece puzzle

INTELLECTUAL

Does your child:

- ask "why" questions
- try to figure out an explanation for things that puzzle him
- follow simple directions, such as "put your cup in the sink and napkin in the trash"

Does your child know (or, at least, has she started to know):

- the alphabet
- the days of the week
- how to count from 1 to 10

Will your child willingly engage in a new activity?

ATTENTION SPAN

Can your child sit still while you read a short story together? Will your child stick with a difficult exercise?

SOCIALIZATION

- Can your child share toys and take turns?

✎ Does she play regularly with other children (may be siblings)?

✎ Can she play well with other children (or at least one)?

✎ Does she know the appropriate ways to express anger (she uses her "words, not fists," may still occasionally lose control)?

INDEPENDENCE

Can your child separate from you for the length of the school day? Can your child:

✎ dress himself (even if some assistance may be necessary)

✎ wash his face and hands

✎ use the toilet on his own

✎ play by himself (i.e., entertain himself, for at least 15 minutes)

Does your child take pride in his work?

Prep for Success?

Should you tutor your child in skills? Not exactly. To a certain extent a child is either developmentally ready or not, and no amount of coaching will make him ready before his time.

On the other hand, if you notice that there are gaps in his knowledge (for example he doesn't know his home address or telephone number), certainly you can practice this information. **But if he is resistant, or just doesn't seem to "get it,"** then back off and wait.

Here are some ways you can encourage his skills development.

LARGE-MOTOR SKILLS

1. Provide opportunities and space where your child can run, climb, skip, hop, etc.
2. Play ball with your youngster including throwing and catching, as well as kickball.
3. Offer the opportunity to practice biking.

SMALL-MOTOR SKILLS

1. Have your child trace around his own hand or other objects.

2. Practice scissors skills by cutting Play-Doh.
3. Encourage block building.
4. Offer increasingly more complicated puzzles, with more and smaller pieces.

COMMUNICATION SKILLS

1. Talk about whatever activity you and your child are doing.
2. Make up stories or recount family adventures.
3. Read together and then discuss the books.
4. Discuss topics of general interest.
5. Use rhymes and wordplay to help your child recognize similar sounds. For example, "What's your number? Cu-cu-cumber. Where do you live? Under the bridge."

SOCIAL SKILLS

1. Make sure your child has the opportunity to play with other children. Often one-on-one play is easier than a group setting.
2. Model good behavior by using polite words such as "please," "thank you," and "excuse me," as well as caring skills and respect for both children and adults.

ACADEMIC SKILLS

1. Assign your child regular chores: It builds self-esteem and teaches math and/or reading concepts. For example, setting the table, giving each place setting a fork, knife, spoon, teaches one-to-one correspondence, which is an important math concept. Pairing socks in the laundry is a fun way to learn classification and sorting.
2. Have your child: make up the shopping list (don't worry about the spelling errors); clip coupons for products used by your family from the newspaper (improves small-motor skills); and match product to coupon in the store (one-to-one correspondence).
3. Make your own books and have your child dictate a story. He can then act as his own illustrator.
4. Encourage problem solving by answering the child's "why," with the response, "Why do you think?"

Kindergarten Readiness Is More than a Date

Don't be intimidated by the calendar. Just because your child meets the cutoff date for kindergarten in your district doesn't mean that she should enter elementary school in September. You need to respond to your child's educational, social, and emotional needs, and match the appropriate program to her developmental level.

Nor should you assume that just because your child has a "late birthday," one that is close to the cutoff date, that he is not ready for kindergarten. It is generally the parents of boys with late fall birthdays, who agonize over whether an additional year in preschool wouldn't make their son better equipped to deal with the "pressures" of "real school."

When deciding whether your child is ready for kindergarten, you'll want to seek the opinions of your child's preschool teacher, as well as the professionals in the elementary school he will be attending. (Most public schools have a screening process to determine a child's readiness; private schools have a more elaborate testing procedure.) You might even choose to see an outside consultant such as an educational psychologist for an independent evaluation. **But don't underestimate your own intuition as parents.** You see your child in another, equally important context.

The Birthday Debate

Since any cutoff date is by definition arbitrary, you can see how important it is to individualize the decision. Of course, you may not have any choice if you choose to enroll your child in a private kindergarten. The school may not only have a cutoff date (which is frequently earlier than the public school date), but may strongly encourage parents of children with birthdays close to that cutoff date to wait another year. One family was surprised when they discovered that their son with a July birthday was the youngest in his private-school class. The school's cutoff date for incoming kindergartners was a birthday before October 1. But the administration routinely encouraged families of boys with August and

September birthdays to wait another year. In fact, it was not unusual for children to enter public kindergarten for a year and then enter the private school kindergarten for the following year.

A study by The National Association for the Education of Young Children makes clear that the issue should not be whether or not the child is "young" for the class. The problem lies in the fact that the academic demands of most kindergartens are inappropriate for young children. Districts are insisting on older kindergartners because the expectations and teaching methods are not developmentally appropriate for five-year-olds.

Why Parents Worry

Nonetheless, parents must make a decision about their child's ability to cope with—flourish in—the kindergarten they find in their neighborhood. The concerns are both academic and social.

Will he be the youngest in his class? The last one to lose a tooth or learn to tie his shoes? Will he be the shortest in the class and the last to be chosen for teams? Will she be more immature than her classmates? One teacher complained to a father about his daughter's inability to sit still for a long period of time. But the child had a birthday close to the cutoff date and was more than eight months younger than many of her classmates. Her attention span was normal for her chronological age, but shorter than her classmates'. How will entry age impact a child's social, emotional, physical, and intellectual development?

What Does the Research Say?

Studies on the long- and short-term effect of entry age on school success have netted mixed results. There are landmark studies to support the theory that kindergarten tends to be more difficult for younger children. One study found that children with learning difficulties in kindergarten and first grade often had "a July to December birth date, late maturation, and other characteristics in common" (Donofrio, 1977). Throughout elementary school, late birth date children, especially boys, were more frequently referred for help with academic problems (DiPasquale, Moule & Flewelling, 1980). And the long-term damaging academic effects of early kindergarten entry have been charted through middle school and beyond.

On the other hand, several other important studies have shown that "the differences due to age are small and disappear with time," often by third grade (National Association of Early Childhood Specialists in State Departments of Education, 1987).

What Do Other Parents Say?

The anecdotal evidence, from other parents and teachers, is also mixed. You will inevitably hear from some parents whose child had a December 31 birthday and "did just fine;" as well as those who maintain that waiting the extra year "was the best gift I could give my child."

One mother explained her decision to wait a year before enrolling her son (birth date December 26) in kindergarten. "Whenever he had problems in school, at least I knew it wasn't because I had pushed him too hard before he was ready." But this same mother did enroll her younger son (birth date November 12) the year he was eligible. "He did have some problems being one of the youngest in the class, but it just happened to turn out that there were several other boys in the class who also had late birthdays." Then she added with a smile; "Still, I bet even when he finishes medical school I'll be second-guessing myself and asking if he would be first in his class if we had waited the extra year."

What Are Your Options?

If you decide not to enroll your child in kindergarten, you have several options. You could choose to have him remain in preschool for another year; opt for a transition class; or enroll in kindergarten with the intention of repeating the class, either in the same school or in another school.

Staying in Preschool

One option is to have your child remain in a four-year-olds class in preschool for another year. If the teachers and director agree, your child could remain in the school. If not, you could enroll your child in the four-year-olds class in another program. It would be best, if the school is large enough to have more than one four-year-olds class, to switch teachers for the second year so that your child has a different experience, even if the curriculum is similar.

The advantage of staying in the same school is that your child and your family are working with people who already know you. The teachers have the benefit of your child's history. If your child is comfortable in the environment, there is none of the tension of adjustment or separation anxiety. Furthermore, if you change schools and enroll your child in a different four-year-olds program, that could mean that he ends up going to three different schools in three years: preschool A, preschool B, and then kindergarten.

On the other hand, if you believe that the program at your current preschool is not appropriate for your child to remain, but you are concerned that she is not ready for kindergarten, you could consider enrolling her in another preschool. Children are often more flexible than we think, and a strong professional staff should help a child adjust to a new situation. One little girl, birth date December 26, entered a 3-year-olds class when she was two years, nine months; entered a 4-year-olds class when she was three years, nine months; and when her parents decided that they wanted to wait before enrolling her in kindergarten, was enrolled in a different preschool that had an "older fours" class, designed for children who were at least four years, six months when school began in September.

Whether your child remains in the same school or switches preschools, discuss the decision with the school's director and ask:

1. Does the school believe an additional year is sometimes helpful and why?
2. Has the school ever had children remain for an additional year? What have been the results of this additional year?
3. How do they help these children feel good about remaining in preschool?
4. Are they prepared to enrich the curriculum for children who are ready for new challenges?

If you are changing schools, be sure to ask:

How does the staff help new children adjust to school, especially when the child is entering the school as a four-year-old and many of the students have already been together for at least a year?

Not Kindergarten, but Not Preschool Either

Some communities have public schools with transition classes, programs especially designed for children who are not ready for kindergarten, but have completed the four-year-olds class in pre-school. Sometimes called *prekindergarten*, they may offer your child a more enriching experience, with more emphasis on academics, but still with a developmental approach to young children.

Other school systems have *pre-first or transition classes*, which are appropriate for children who have *completed* kindergarten, but who are judged not ready for a mainstream first-grade class.

If your child has been identified as learning disabled, check with your school district. Some offer classes specifically designed for children with speech or learning delays, with the goal that the child will then be mainstreamed into a regular classroom the following year (either a kindergarten or first grade). Your child may have to be tested to qualify for these programs.

If your concern is a question of maturity, rather than any specific learning disability, you will want to make sure that any program you choose will be developmentally appropriate for your child.

Some private schools also have pre-K programs, specifically designed for children with "late birthdays." Since private schools frequently have an earlier cutoff date than public schools (many as early as July 1 for boys), there is a greater demand for these transition classes. Here's the school history of one little boy, birth-date August 15. When he was two, he was enrolled in a "Mommy and Me" program at a local Y for two mornings a week. The next year, he entered a private preschool, which had programs for threes, fours, and a pre-K program for fives. Of the 10 boys in his pre-K class, five went to kindergarten and five entered first grade. His parents enrolled him, now age six, in the kindergarten class of a private K-12 school.

> **TIP:** Remember that children change a lot in just six months. Your child may mature dramatically over the course of the summer before kindergarten begins.

Taking a Chance

If you are on the fence about whether or not your child is ready for kindergarten, you may decide that it's worth the risk, especially if you believe the kindergarten program offers a supportive environment.

One family was concerned about their son's kindergarten entry because he appeared to be immature. There were no learning or speech difficulties, but he still had difficulty with separation and socialization. They made an appointment with an educational psychologist to discuss their apprehensions. One of the problems was that the parents did not like their current preschool, but worried about the effect on their son of going to three different schools in three years.

The psychologist suggested an alternative. The local public school offered kindergarten classes, as well as a combined kindergarten–first-grade class. She suggested to the parents that they enroll the little boy in the regular kindergarten class, and if, at the end of the kindergarten year, the teacher and parents felt the child was not ready for first grade, then he could enter the combined K-1 class for two more years. In this way, the child would make only one switch to a new school, it would be a familiar environment, and the teachers and administration could follow his progress over the years. The child matured during that kindergarten year and all the parties decided in the spring that he was ready for a regular first-grade class.

How to Explain Your Decision to Your Child

How you and the preschool teachers present the decision to your child will determine, in large measure, how your child accepts the plan. Be positive and reassuring. Most of all, you don't want your child to believe that somehow he has failed. Speak matter-of-factly, without voicing any concerns or doubts. *If you feel sure of the decision, so will your child*. Try to be brief. Your child may have questions and you'll want to answer them, but a lengthy explanation may only confuse him.

Here's how you might phrase the decision. "When you were only 12 months old you took your very first step. But your friend, Jack, didn't walk until he was 15 months old. Now, of course, both of you walk, and run, and climb. Well, school is the same way. Just because Jack is going to kindergarten this fall doesn't mean it's the right time for you to go. Instead, you're going to stay in preschool for another year, this time in Mrs. King's class. You'll go to kindergarten the following year. And here are some of the exciting things you'll be doing in Mrs. King's class . . ."

Your child may need time to process the information. He may come back to you at a later time to ask his questions. He also may be angry or frustrated, demanding that he go on to kindergarten with his friends. Don't be defensive about your decision, but acknowledge that he may be angry or hurt. "I know that you would like to go to school with Jack, but Daddy and I don't think that kindergarten is the right place for you next year. But we'll make sure that you still have time to play with Jack outside of school." Don't insist that he will make new friends (even though that is true). He likes the ones he has.

As with many parenting experiences, you need to make clear to your child that while you can sympathize with his feelings, "this is a Mommy and Daddy decision." It is reassuring to a child that a grown-up is in charge.

Saying Good-bye to Preschool

If your child is going on to kindergarten, you will want to mark the end of her preschool experience. Even if you have decided that your child is not going to kindergarten, it marks the end of *this* four-year-olds class.

Some preschools have graduation ceremonies at the end of the four-year-olds class, others may not; in any case, it's a good idea to have a small family celebration. It doesn't have to be fancy, perhaps just lunch at the local pizza parlor or an ice-cream cake after dinner. It's an acknowledgment that your child is growing up and moving on to a new exciting place—and that you are proud of her. It also gives closure to the experience and helps prepare her for the next step. Remember, if she has been in preschool for two or even three years, that is three-fifths of her life!

The four-year-olds teacher will probably talk about kindergarten with her students. She may role-play some of the experiences that your child may encounter, for example, the bus ride if you live in a district that buses children to school. You may also see several of the four-year-olds "playing school" during free time.

You'll want to prepare your child as well. If your local kindergarten does not have an orientation program for incoming kindergartners, take your youngster to the school before classes begin. It's reassuring to a youngster to see that her parents are comfortable in the elementary school. It tells her that this is a safe place to be.

Many of the steps you used to prepare her for preschool can be used again in preparation for kindergarten. See Suggested Reading chapter for books that you can read together before school begins.

Getting Ready for Elementary School

You have been encouraging your child since birth to value and love learning. You've made it clear that education is a priority in your family and that everyone, grown-ups included, can always learn something new. Here are some other tips to make sure that your child is enthusiastic and excited about beginning her elementary school career.

1. Let your child know that you are excited that she is beginning kindergarten.
2. Tell your child that you have confidence that he is ready to enter kindergarten.
3. Give him more experiences, such as play dates at other children's homes and visits with grandparents or relatives, where he can see that he can operate independently of you.
4. Actively seek out new learning experiences for yourself—and some that you can share together. For example, take an adult

LOOKING BACK HELPS THE PRESENT

Sometimes, it's helpful to take your child to visit her preschool after she begins kindergarten. It's reassuring to see old friends (her teachers), and it's a reminder of how much she has grown. She can see the difference between her "old school" and her "new school." It's also a quiet reminder to your child that she was successful in school before—and that she can be successful again.

education class and let your child see that education is a lifelong process.

5. Let your child see how reading and writing help you in life. For example, let her see you look up a recipe or go to the encyclopedia to find the answer to a question she has asked. You want her to see that education is not only fun, but has a practical value as well.

6. Encourage respect for teachers, schools, and education in general. Talk about the important role teachers have in our society. This reinforces the idea that going to school is a special, important activity.

Questions and Answers

Q: My son has a late September birthday. He is very smart and enjoys the half-day preschool he attends, but I am worried about sending him to kindergarten in the fall. He is very shy, and I am concerned whether he is mature enough to handle an all-day kindergarten. Also, his younger brother is only two years behind him, so if I hold the older one back, should I also retain the younger one to keep the spacing?

A: You have to separate several issues. First, is *this* child ready for kindergarten? Just because he has a late birthday or is shy does not mean he won't succeed in kindergarten. What do his preschool teachers recommend?

Second, the half-day versus full-day program will probably

be an adjustment for most of the children in the class. If your child tends to tire at the end of the day, limit his after-school activities and plan an earlier bedtime. He will adjust, but you may find him very tired at the end of a long day.

Third, you have to make decisions about each child individually. While whatever you choose will impact on the other family members, you need to focus on how the educational decision will help this child. Your younger child may need to wait before entering kindergarten—but only if he needs the time, not because you want to maintain the spacing in the family.

Q: **My daughter is very bright. She has been reading since she was three years old. Do you think she should skip kindergarten and enter a first-grade class? I don't want her to be bored.**

A: Education is more than reading, writing, and arithmetic. You want your child to be well educated and well adjusted. Talk to the school psychologist, but in general, most experts suggest that skipping grades leads to more problems than it solves, especially as your child gets older. Better that you add enrichment to a program that is age appropriate, than to try to adjust the socialization process for a young, but very bright child.

Ask the kindergarten teacher what provisions are made for the child who is already reading. A good teacher will provide enrichment for those students who are ready for a bigger challenge. Check out whether your district has a program for the gifted.

Don't forget that enrichment doesn't only come from the school. You can provide learning-rich activities at home, as well. But remember not to focus solely on the academic. Your child needs to have time just to be a kid. It doesn't matter if the children she plays with are her intellectual equals or not.

Q: **We've just moved here and I've heard that the school my son will attend has two kindergarten teachers. One is supposed to be fabulous, the other is nice but disorganized. How can I make sure that my child gets the really good teacher?**

A: In most school districts, you can't specifically request a teacher. You can, however, speak *in code*, where you try to describe the kind of teacher you want so specifically that only one teacher would fill the bill. For example, ask for an appointment with the principal. You might say: "I think my son will do better in a highly structured, organized classroom with a teacher who has a lot of experience with children who have just moved to the district and may be having trouble adjusting." You haven't mentioned names, but you've made your choice very clear.

But a word about teachers in general. Sometimes a teacher's bad reputation isn't deserved or at least has to be understood in context. Sometimes it's just that a teacher has had a bad year. She could have personal difficulties (a death in the family or a divorce), and it's not unusual, if unfortunate, that her work suffers. But when the crisis has passed, she becomes a better teacher. Sometimes the chemistry of the class makes for a difficult year. One veteran teacher who had enjoyed a good reputation for years was suddenly being considered a shrew. If you spoke to parents from two different years, you'd think you were discussing two different teachers. But a closer look at the class that had produced the poor reputation revealed a difficult class with several very troubled children. Any teacher would have had a tough time. And sometimes, you have to consider the source of the criticism. What one parent finds objectionable, another may prefer. Some families like an open classroom; others would prefer a more traditional class environment with a more traditional teacher.

Finally, unfortunately, your child may encounter a poor teacher or two during her school career. In those cases, when you can make a switch (which is usually very difficult), of course, you would. But if you can't, you will need to supplement the school education with additional help at home. And you will want to support your child during a difficult time.

Q: My son likes school, but is fearful of the bus ride (the children in this district are all bused). Should I drive him to

school? I could rearrange my schedule, but it would be easier if he took the bus.

A: Your ultimate goal should be for your child to ride the bus. Why? Because the other children in the district all go to school this way, and he will feel better about himself if he can too.

First, try to determine what is making your child fearful? Does he get carsick, so any bus ride would make him worried? If so, talk to your doctor about medication and the best place to sit on the bus in order to avoid motion sickness (generally in the front of the bus and near an open window).

Have older children told him stories about the "wild" bus ride—and are these tales actually true? If so, talk to the district about how the school controls the children on the bus and whether additional monitors are needed.

Prepare him for this new experience as you would any other—through talking, reading books, and role-playing. Many districts take new kindergartners on a test run before school opens. If your district does not, ask if your child can at least meet the driver and see the bus before he must take his first ride.

Try to arrange to have your child sit with another kindergartner on the bus, at least for the first few days. Or you might ask an older neighborhood child (even offer to pay) if she would look out for your son on the bus.

One mother tried a different variation for a few days. Her child took the bus—but she met him at the school and walked him to his class. It gave him an opportunity to "settle down" before school began.

Riding the school bus is another "educational" experience. You are looking for ways to help your child succeed—and when he does, it will be a boost to his self-esteem.

APPENDIX 1

Preschool Evaluation Sheet

Name of School _____

Director _____

Address _____

Telephone _____

Accreditation_____

Type of School _____

Religious Affiliation _____

Tuition _____

Visit_____

First Impressions

Is the preschool:

cheerful _____

bright _____

spacious_____

clean_____

orderly _____

well-lit_____

noise level (quiet hum?) _____

Does the staff seem:

to interact with the children _____

affectionate _____

overworked _____

distracted_____
Do the children seem:
happy _____
interested_____
busy _____
to interact with each other
to interact with staff _____

Physical Layout

Overall appearance of classrooms _____

Book Corner   Inviting? _____
How many Books?: _____ Age appropriate?_____
Toilets: Easily accessible? _____
Child-sized?_____
Science Center _____
Blocks_____
Dress-Up Area _____
Art Supplies _____
Water/Sand Table _____
Toys
Are there enough toys for the number of children?_____
Are there duplicates of very popular toys? _____
Do children have to wait long to play with certain toys? _____
Are the toys well-maintained and clean? _____
Comments_____
_____
_____
_____

Playground

Easily accessible? _____
Well-maintained? _____
Size-appropriate equipment? _____
Fenced? _____
Are there riding toys? _____
How many? _____

On a scale of 1 to 5, with 5 representing the best, rate the playground equipment for variety, safety, interest, and accessibility for young children. _____

Teachers

Ratio of teachers/assistants to students _____
Educational Credentials _____

On a scale of 1 to 5, with 5 representing the best, how would you evaluate the teaching staff? _____
Comments _____

_____

Outside Specialists _____

_____

Children on a scale of 1 to 5, with 5 representing the best, do the students appear to be:

Engaged in interesting activities _____
Happy _____
Well-supervised _____
Playing with each other _____
Talking with each other _____
Talking with teachers _____
Comments _____

_____

Health and Safety

Is at least one person on staff trained in CPR and have a Red Cross first aid certificate? _____
Are emergency fire drills held? _____
Are there smoke detectors and fire extinguishers in place? _____
Are all visitors screened before entering the school? _____
Is there a clear dismissal policy? _____
Is written permission needed before releasing your child to anyone other than a parent or authorized caregiver? _____

How is traffic around the school organized? _____

Does the school maintain a strict immunization policy? _____

Are emergency numbers clearly posted? _____

General Comments and Observations _____

APPENDIX 2

Recommended Childhood Immunization Schedule United States, January–December 1997

Vaccines[1] are listed under the routinely recommended sages. Bars indicate range of acceptable ages for vaccination. Shaded bars indicate catch-up vaccination; at 11–12 years of age, hepatitis B vaccine should be administered to children not previously vaccinated, and Varicella vaccine should be administered to children not previously vaccinated who lack a reliable history of chicken pox.

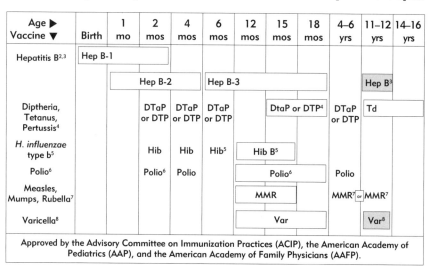

Approved by the Advisory Committee on Immunization Practices (ACIP), the American Academy of Pediatrics (AAP), and the American Academy of Family Physicians (AAFP).

[1] This schedule indicates the recommended age for routine administration of currently licensed childhood vaccines. Some combination vaccines are available and may be used whenever adminisration of all components of the vaccine is

indicated. Providers should consult the manufacturers' package inserts for detailed recommendations.

[2] **Infants born to HBsAg-negative mothers** should receive 2.5 µg of Merck vaccine (Recombivax HB) or 10 µg of SmithKline Beecham (SB) vaccine (Engerix-B). The 2nd dose should be administered ≥ 1 mo after the 1st dose.

Infants born to HBsAg-positive mothers should receive 0.5 ml hepatitis B immune globulin (HBIG) within 12 hrs of birth, and either 5 µg of Merck vaccine (Recombivax HB) or 10 µg of SB vaccine (Engerix-B) at a separate site. The 2nd dose is recommended at 1–2 mos of age and the 3rd dose at 6 mos of age.

Infants born to mothers whose HBsAg status is unknown should receive either 5 µg of Merck vaccine (Recombinvax HB) or 10 µg of SB vaccine (Engerix-B) within 12 hrs of birth. The 2nd dose of vaccine is recommended at 1 mo of age and the 3rd dose at 6 mos of age. Blood should be drawn at the time of delivery to determine the mother's HBsAg status; if it is positive, the infant should receive HVIG as soon as possible (no later than 1 week of age). The dosage and timing of subsequent vaccine doses should be based upon the mother's HBsAg status.

[3] Children and adolescents who have not been vaccinated against hepatitis B in infancy may begin the series during any childhood visit. Those who have not previously received 3 doses of hepatitis B vaccine should initiate or complete the series during the 11–12 year-old visit. The 2nd dose should be administered at least 1 mo after the 1st dose, and the 3rd dose should be administered at least 4 mos after the 1st dose and at least 2 mos after the 2nd dose.

[4] DTaP (diphtheria and tetanus toxoids and acellular pertussis vaccine) is the preferred vaccine for all doses in the vaccination series, including completion of the series in children who have received ≥ 1 dose of whole-cell DTP vaccine. Whole-cell DTP is an acceptable alternative to DTaP. The 4th dose of DTaP may be administered as early as 12 months of age, provided 6 months have elapsed since the 3rd dose, and if the child is considered unlikely to return at 15–18 mos of age. Td (tetanus and diphtheria toxoids, absorbed, for adult use) is recommended at 11–12 years of age if at least 5 years have elapsed since the last dose of DTP, DTaP, or DT. Subsequent routine Td boosters are recommended every 10 years.

[5] Three *H. influenzae* type b (Hib) conjugate vaccines are licensed for infant use. If PRPOMP (PedvaxHIB [Merck]) is administered at 2 and 4 mos of age, a dose at 6 mos is not required. After completing the primary series, any Hib conjugate vaccine may be used as a booster.

[6] Two poliovirus vaccines are currently licensed in the US: inactivated poliovirus vaccine (IPV) and oral poliovirus vaccine (OPV). The following schedules are all acceptable by the ACIP, the AAP, and the AAFP, and parents and providers may choose among them:

    1. IPV at 2 and 4 mos; OPV at 12–18 mos and 4–6 yr

2. IPV at 2, 4, 12–18 mos, and 4–6 yr
3. OPV at 2, 4, 6–18 mos, and 4–6 yr

The ACIP routinely recommends schedule 1. IPV is the only poliovirus vaccine recommended for immunocompromised persons and their household contacts.

[7] The 2nd dose of MMR is routinely recommended at 4–6 yrs of age or at 11–12 yrs of age, but may be administered during any visit, provided at least 1 month has elapsed since receipt of the 1st dose and that both doses are administered at or after 12 months of age.

[8] Susceptible children may receive Varicella vaccine (Var) at any visit after the first birthday, and those who lack a reliable history of chickenpox should be immunized during the 11–12 year-old visit. Children ≥13 years of age should receive 2 doses, at least 1 mo apart.

Immuniztion Protects Children

Regular checkups at your pediatrician's office or local health clinic are an important way to keep children healthy.

By making sure that your child gets immunized on time, you can provide the best available defense against many dangerous childhood diseases. Immunizations protect children against: Hepatitis B. polio, measles, mumps, rubella (German measles), pertussis (whooping cough), diphtheria, tetanus (lockjaw), *Haemophilus influenzae* type b, and chickenpox. All of these immunizations need to be given before children are 2 years old in order for them to be protected during their most vulnerable period. Are your child's immunizations up-to-date?

The chart . . . of this fact sheet includes immunization recommendations from the American Academy of Pediatrics. Remember to keep track of your child's immunizations—it's the only way you can be sure your child is up-to-date. Also, check with your pediatrician or health clinic at each visit to find out if your child needs any booster shots or if any new vaccines have been recommended since this schedule was prepared.

If you don't have a pediatrician, call your local health department. Public health clinics usually have supplies of vaccine and may give shots free.

The information contained in this publication should not be used as a substitute for the medical care and advice of your pediatrician. There may be variations in treatment that your pediatrician may recommend based on individual facts and circumstances.

APPENDIX 3

Resources

Organizations that can provide information and help with early childhood education issues.

Child Care Action Campaign
nonprofit advocacy group; provides information to business leaders, educators, legislators, and parents about the need for good quality child care for all families
330 Seventh Avenue, 17th Floor
New York, NY 10001
212–239–0138

ERIC Clearinghouse on Elementary and Early Childhood Education
provides information for educators and parents on development, education, and care of children from birth through early adolescence
University of Illinois, Champaign-Urbana
Children's Research Center
51 Gerty Drive
Champaign, IL 61820–7469
217–333–1386; 800–583–4135
e-mail: ERICEECE@UIUC.edu

The International Nanny Association
nonprofit educational organization for nannies and those who educate, place, employ, and support professional in-home child-care providers.

Provides, for a fee, a directory of training programs, nanny placement agencies, and special services.
900 Haddon Avenue, Suite 438
Collingswood, NJ 08108
609–858–0808

National Academy of Early Childhood Programs
independent accrediting agency, affiliated with NAEYC
1834 Connecticut Avenue NW
Washington, DC 20009

National Association for Family Child Care (NAFCC)
accredits family day-care homes; will send a list of day-care referral agencies and day-care provider support groups in your state and local area.
Send a stamped, self-addressed envelope to:
NAFCC Accreditation
P.O. Box 161489
Fort Worth, TX 76161

National Association for the Education of Young Children (NAEYC)
provides information on child-care options; an excellent source of publications
1509 16th Street NW
Washington, DC 20036–1826
800–424–2460

National Association of Child Care Resources and Referral Agencies
umbrella group that can provide information on local resources
2116 Campus Drive SE
Rochester, MN 55904
507–287–2020

Association of Waldorf Schools of North America
3911 Bannister Road
Fair Oaks, CA 95628
916–961–0927

Web Sites for Parent Support Groups

ON AMERICA ONLINE

Keyword: **Momsonline**
Keyword: **Parent Soup**

ON THE INTERNET

Parents Place
http://www.parentsplace.com

Parents Helping Parents
organization devoted to parents who have children with special needs due to illness, accidents, birth defects, allergies, learning problems, family problems, family stress

http://www.php.com

National Parent Information Network
provides information and fosters an exchange of parenting materials
http://ericps.ed.uiuc.edu/npin/npinhome.html

GLOSSARY

Child-Centered Program A child's own curiosity propels the curriculum. He discovers and learns at his own pace, using the toys, materials and setting, and interaction with peers, with little teacher direction.

Cooperative Parents share the preschool cost and responsibilities (administrative and financial) for the program. May range from completely parent run to parent volunteers helping defray some costs, but primarily run by professional staff. Generally less expensive than private preschool program.

Day-Care Center Usually refers to a institution that offers full-day care, often 12 months a year. May care for a range of ages, from infancy through kindergarten, and offer after-school care for older children as well. Does not indicate what kind of curriculum is followed.

Developmental Approach Curriculum based on age-appropriate play, activities, and materials.

Head Start The oldest, federally funded free preschool program for disadvantaged youngsters.

Maria Montessori Italian physician-educator (1870–1952), believed in a developmental approach to learning, but within a specially prepared environment and with teachers who have been trained in the Montessori method.

Jean Piaget Swiss psychologist (1896–1980) whose educational theories emphasized "developmentally appropriate" activities, rather than focusing on chronological age and that children "learn through doing."

Pre-K program   A subsidized educational program in local school districts for disadvantaged or disabled children.

Preschool   Also refers to nursery schools and play schools. Generally part-time programs, mornings or afternoons. Does not indicate the type of curriculum followed.

Progressive Schools   Usually identified with John Dewey. This educational movement began around the start of the 20th century. Child-centered pedagogy with emphasis on learning by doing, hands-on activities; active learning rather than passive learning.

Stanford-Binet   Standardized test sometimes used in screening children for admission to private preschools.

Teacher-Directed Program   Teacher controls the pace and activities of the day. Much more formal classroom instruction.

Waldorf or Rudolf Steiner Schools   Rudolf Steiner, an early 20th-century Austrian philosopher, developed an educational theory responsive to the developmental phases in childhood, encouraging creativity and free-thinking. Central to the curriculum are art, music, gardening, and foreign languages. All subjects are taught through artistic mediums. Currently 600 schools in 32 countries.

Wechsler Preschool and Primary Scale of Intelligence (WPPSI)   Standardized test sometimes used in screening children for admission to private preschools.

SUGGESTED READING ON PRESCHOOLS

Brenner, Barbara. *The Preschool Handbook*. New York: Pantheon Books, 1990.

Craig, Judi. *What Happened at School Today*. New York: Hearst Books, 1994.

Eisenberg, Arlene, Heidi E. Murkoff, and Sandee E. Hathaway. *What to Expect the Toddler Years*. New York: Workman Publishing, 1994.

Elkind, David. *Miseducation*, New York: Alfred A. Knopf, 1988.

Galinsky, Ellen and Judy David. *The Preschool Years*. New York: Times Books, 1988.

Kutner, Lawrence. *Toddlers and Preschoolers*. New York: William Morrow and Company, 1994.

Miller, Jo Ann, and Susan Weissman. *The Parents' Guide to Daycare*. New York: Bantam Books, 1986.

Townsend-Butterworth, Diana. *Your Child's First School*. New York: Walker and Company, 1992.

Books to Read to Children about Preschool

Ahlberg, Janet, and Allan. *Starting School*. New York: Puffin Books, 1990.

Berenstain, Stan, and Jan. *The Berenstain Bears Go to School*. New York: Random House, 1978.

Cohen, Miriam. *Will I Have a Friend?*. New York: Macmillan, 1967.

Conlin, Susan, and Susan Friedman. *Let's Talk about Feelings: Nathan's Day at Preschool*. Seattle: Parenting Press, 1991.

Day, Alexandra. *Carl Goes to Daycare*. New York: Farrar, Strauss, Giroux, 1993.

Demuth, Patricia Brennan. *Busy Day at Day Care Head to Toe*. New York: Dutton Children's Books, 1996.

Hoffman, Phyllis. *Meatball*. New York: HarperCollins, 1991.

Johnson, Dolores. *What Will Mommy Do When I'm at School?* New York: Macmillan, 1990.

Magorian, Michelle. *Who's Going to Take Care of Me?* New York: Harper & Row, 1990.

Rockwell, Harlow. *My Nursery School*. New York: Greenwillow, 1976.

Rogers, Fred. *Going to Day Care*. New York: Putnam, 1985.

Tompert, Ann. *Will You Come Back for Me?* Niles, Ill.: A. Whitman, 1988.

Valens, Amy. *Jesse's Daycare*. Boston: Houghton Mifflin, 1990.

Wolde, Gunilla. *Betsy's First Day at Daycare*. New York: Random House, 1976.

INDEX

Italicized page numbers refer to information in boxes.